**CORNWALL COUNTY COUNCIL
LIBRARIES AND ARTS DEPARTMENT**

GW00455035

A CORNISH INHERITANCE

The Harveys of Chacewater

-o-o-o-o-o-o-

David Gore

Published by the author at
The Red House, Lower Basildon, Berkshire RG8 9NG

1997

Front Cover Picture: Carn Galver mine, just one of many ruined Engine Houses. They stand like giant tombstones, melancholy memorials to Cornwall's great mining tradition and the 'old men' of past generations whose arduous labour in the face of danger and privation brought prosperity to Cornwall for nearly two centuries.

Back Cover Picture: The 'Harvey' window in St Paul's, Chacewater (page 40). The window which was installed in 1931 is dedicated as follows:-

"To the Glory of God and in loving memory of
Sophia and Richard Williams Harvey and of their children"

First published in 1997 by:
David Gore,
The Red House,
Lower Basildon,
Berkshire RG8 9NG   Tel: 01491-671300

Copyright © David Gore 1997

Printed and bound by Antony Rowe Ltd, Bumper's Farm, Chippenham, Wiltshire SN14 6LH

Front cover picture © Bob Croxford, Atmospheres, Mullion, Cornwall TR12 7DF

British Library Cataloguing in Publication Data.
A catalogue record for this book is available from the British Library

ISBN 0 9530912 0 1   **1394**

CONTENTS

LIST OF ILLUSTRATIONS

LIST OF PEDIGREES

ACKNOWLEDGEMENTS

I have to thank many people who helped me to complete this brief history of the Chacewater Harveys and some of their Cornish relations. The bulk of the material, that on the multifarious branches of the Harvey family itself, was made available to me by Rosemary Morgan of West Wickham, Richard Harvey of Double Bay, New South Wales, and Bill Pellew-Harvey of Mill Valley, California, who all generously allowed me to use the product of their own family researches and later reviewed my text. I am also grateful to them for permitting their own stories to be told in the Supplement as a means of bringing this 'history' up to date.

I would also like to thank the following, all of whom gave me either material, advice or encouragement, and many of them all three:
Liz Addie of Towcester, Sarah Apps of Tooting Bec, Alison Banister of Wimbledon, Mike and Ann Birley of Marlborough, Audrey Bray of Rosudgeon, Justin Brooke of Marazion, Dr Andrew Causey of Manchester University, Ian Collins of Lewisham, Richard Hichens of Calenick, Robert Hichens of Flushing, Bernard Jenkin of Chacewater, Sir John Knill of Bathampton, Margaret Le Breton of Weymouth, Stephen Pellew-Harvey of Henley, Vyvyan and the late Ted Pellew-Harvey of Dorchester-on-Thames, Lady Ursula Redwood of Flushing, Jonathan Smalley of Tewkesbury, Anne Stevens of Bampton, Anne Tennent of Totteridge and Rae Williams of Godalming.

I gratefully acknowledge the generous help given me by Gillian Thompson, Trudi Martin and Dave Quensell of the Cornwall Family History Society, by Christine North and her staff at the Cornwall Record Office, by Lt Cdr John Beck of the Falmouth Maritime Museum and by Jane Shanley of Antony Rowe Ltd.

I am also grateful to Robert and Richard Hichens for allowing me to include extracts from the Journal of their ancestor Robert Hichens 1782-1865 in Chapter 7, and to Kate Barker of Curtis Brown for letting me quote from Daphne du Maurier's book *Enchanted Cornwall* in Chapters 1 and 2. In the Supplement the extracts from *Outline, An Autobiography & Other Writings* by Paul Nash (Faber & Faber 1949) are printed by kind permission of Robin Langdon-Davies and John Sibley of the Paul Nash Trust.

PART 1

CORNWALL

-o-o-o-o-o-o-

Look to the rock from which you are hewn,
to the quarry from which you were dug;
look to your father Abraham
and to Sarah who gave you birth:
when I called him he was but one,
I blessed him and made him many.

Isaiah 51 v.1-2

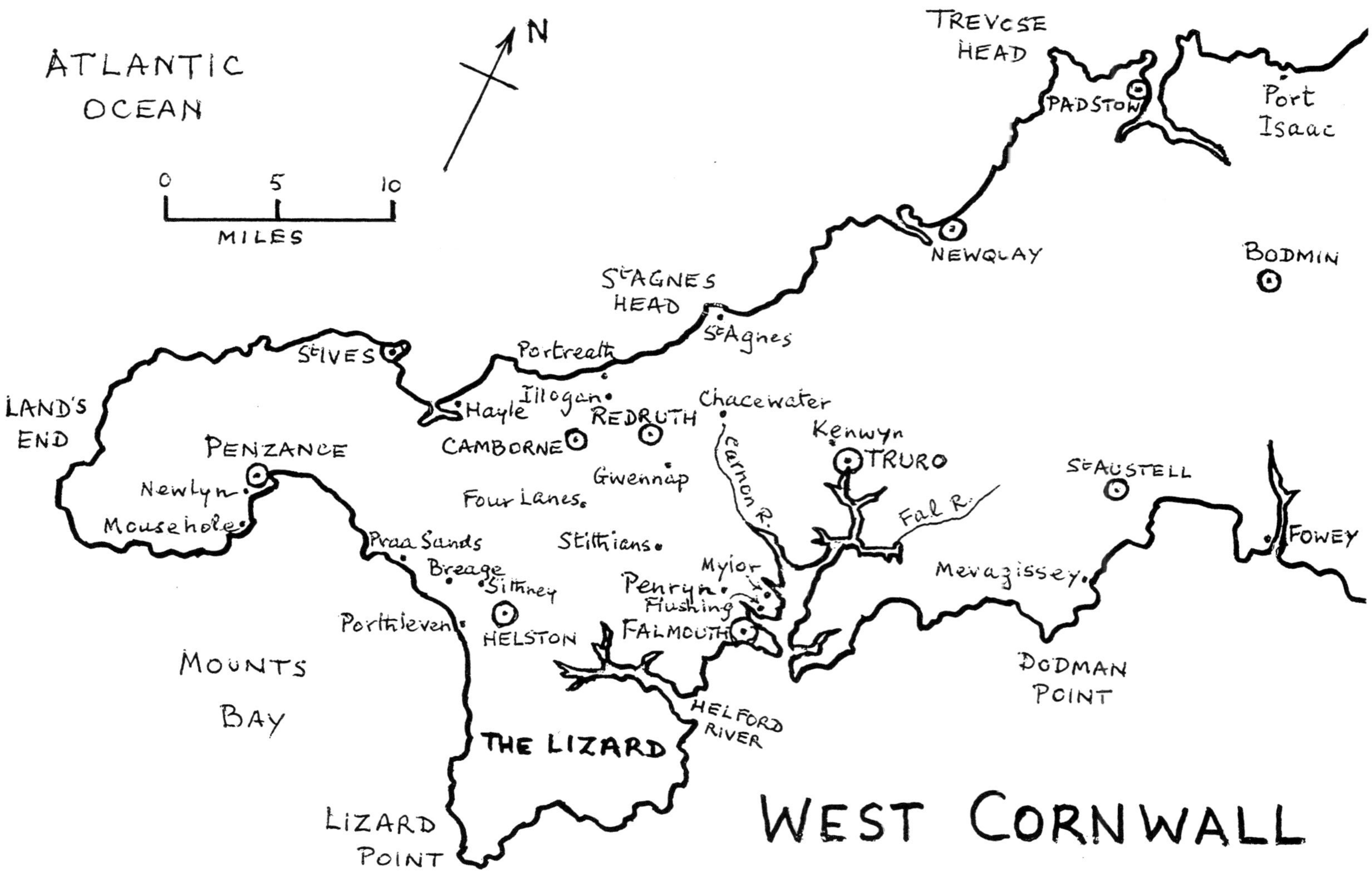
WEST CORNWALL
ATLANTIC
OCEAN
N
0
5
10
MILES
TREVOSE
HEAD
PADSTOW
Port
Isaac
NEWQUAY
BODMIN
St AGNES
HEAD
St Agnes
Portreath
St IVES
LAND'S
END
Illogan
Hayle
REDRUTH
Chacewater
CAMBORNE
Kenwyn
TRURO
St AUSTELL
PENZANCE
Newlyn
Mousehole
Gwennap
Four Lanes
Carnon R.
Fal R.
FOWEY
Stithians
Mylor
Mevagissey
Praa Sands
Breage
Sithney
Penryn
Flushing
Porthleven
HELSTON
FALMOUTH
MOUNTS
BAY
DODMAN
POINT
HELFORD
RIVER
THE LIZARD
LIZARD
POINT

Chapter 1

AN ENCHANTED LAND

This patchwork of a family's history is rather threadbare but has some interesting facets. Despite our best efforts we still know little of individual members of this Harvey family and its branches, beyond the male line of descent from an early 18th century marriage that took place in a mining village on the north coast of Cornwall. Nevertheless here is an attempt to set out some of what we have learned of them against their distinctively Cornish background and the great events, especially in the mining industry, which shaped their lives.

Cornwall which is at the heart of this story has been described as an "enchanted" land. In a way this remote corner of England has a mystical quality about it, stemming from its separate Celtic history, its missionary "saints", strange legends, hidden coves and its comparative isolation over the centuries. It was after all the home of King Arthur, that ethereal hero whom the Cornish have always believed led their resistance to the Anglo-Saxons during the Dark Ages. West Cornwall has the finest prehistoric landscape in Europe, a pagan world of Neolithic burial chambers, Iron Age villages such as 'Carn Euny'; and then there are all those early Christian Celtic crosses and memorial stones, many like 'Mên Scryfa' inscribed in Latin to tribal chiefs of the 6th and 7th centuries, which stand guard across the countryside, each a reminder of Cornwall's ancient past.

Even the brash description by a Londoner on a recent visit to the Cornish coast picks up on the atmosphere of this place apart: "Sleepy little fishing village, scudding clouds, ship's horns spearing the gloom, gnarled monosyllabic seniors mending their nets, the sound of muffled rowlocks, smuggling, coves, women in hoods marching to slack drums, strange local customs - once a month the magistrate is replaced on the bench by the village idiot. They are very independent here; they are still at war with Spain; they stand alone, a little inbred, they all marry their cousins..."

The elemental struggle against wind, rock and sea to carve out a meagre living has helped to shape the Cornish character - described by a visiting Frenchman in the 19th century as "stoicism in the face of great hardship and poverty". The so-called 'reserve' of the Cornishman has no unfriendly intent but was said by Daphne du Maurier to be "something sturdier, more deep-rooted, a self-sufficiency bred in the bone through centuries of independence and being largely his own master, with a natural scepticism and suspicion of the stranger who asks questions". As one of her old Cornish characters said, "we are an ancient race, sir: frank and joyous among ourselves, and especially joyous and childish with our own children, but bred in-and-in and secretive". I am not sure how such characteristics play today with all the visitors that now flock in to the County, but no doubt the Cornish will adapt as they have in the past - slowly!

'Mên Scryfa' (Stone of Writing) was inscribed in Latin. This weathered memorial stone of the 6th century commemorates a chieftain, Rialobran (Royal Raven) son of Cunoval.

Like other Celtic peoples the Cornish have a strong spiritual dimension. Long before St Augustine arrived in Kent to convert the Anglo-Saxons, Cornwall was a refuge for Christianity in a pagan England. Celtic Christianity became firmly established from the 6th century when travelling evangelists started to arrive there from Brittany, Wales and Ireland. These missionary "saints" founded most of Cornwall's churches, and numerous villages, such as Kenwyn (St Keyne), Breage (St Breaca) and St Ives (St Ia), are named after them.

When in 1743 John Wesley and his brothers came riding in to breathe new life into the church, it had never recovered from the Reformation and was suffering from long term neglect and from the materialism of newly affluent miners. Just a mile east of Redruth is the Gwennap Pit, a natural amphitheatre caused by collapsed mine workings where thousands came each year to hear Wesley preach. Methodists still hold an open air service there each Whit-Monday coinciding with one of the biggest attractions of the year, the Redruth fair. In his

46 year long ministry to Cornwall Wesley won over not only the simple country folk but also many of the hard drinking 'tinners' with their reputation for lawlessness. He taught the Cornish to believe again, and a century later they had a bishop and a cathedral in Truro.

The Gwennap Pit near Redruth where thousands came to hear Wesley preach. An annual Whit-Monday service has been held here since 1807.

The peninsula that is Cornwall is seventy miles long and points like a finger out into the Atlantic. It has more than 300 miles of coastline if you count the many creeks and inlets. While the granite cliffs of the north coast are exposed to the full force of the ocean, the south is generally softer, characterised by safe estuaries, such as Falmouth, Fowey and the Helford river, picturesque fishing villages like Mousehole, and beautiful wooded river valleys. Behind the coast there is generally a maze of small green fields with unyielding hedgebanks, narrow roads, sweeps of bracken and then open moorland crowned by granite outcrops twice as old as the Alps. There is seldom a tree in sight from the coastal paths and even the ubiquitous gorse bush has been pruned down by the sea winds. Yet in spring these cliffs and granite headlands become a giant rock garden smothered in wild flowers, bluebells, primroses, violets, and later foxgloves and clumps of pink thrift. On a calm day with the flowers in bloom, the sun shining and the sea is as blue as the Aegean you would not wish to be anywhere else.

Over the centuries Cornishmen and their little ships have set forth from their sheltered harbours on voyages of discovery, voyages to trade, make war, emigrate, sometimes for privateering, piracy or smuggling, and of course to fish. They have often had to fight to protect their cargoes against pirates, particularly from the Barbary Coast, but also from the depredations caused by French and Spanish ships both in time of peace as well as war. British naval history is blazoned with such famous Cornish names as Grenville, Pellew and Boscawen. They, and perhaps also pirates like Carew and the Killigrews, symbolise the courage and buccaneering spirit of the Cornish seamen who held their own and in the process faced the Armada, plundered 'enemy' shipping and raided ports across the Channel. In retaliation Fowey, Looe, Mousehole, Newlyn and Penzance were all at various times sacked or burned by Breton, French or Spanish ships. Life at sea or even in Cornish harbours seems to have been no less hazardous than in its deep mines.

During the 19th century "Fish, Tin and Copper!" used to be the Cornishman's toast to the things on which his livelihood depended. Of the fish, it was pilchards that were vital to the economy. They formed the basic diet of the labouring poor as well as being a staple export. At the end of each summer huge pilchard shoals used to arrive into in-shore waters stretching like cloud shadows across the sea. They brought prosperity to the fishermen of Mevagissey, Polperro, Mousehole and on the north coast Port Isaac, which were the main centres for the industry. Towards the end of the century these shoals dwindled, only partly replaced by mackerel, and with them went the availability of cheap nourishing food. Coinciding as it did with a steep decline in work for miners, it was a further spur to the great Cornish exodus that followed and was to change the face of Cornwall and the lives of the Harveys and many families like them.

Chapter 2

THE RISE AND FALL OF KING COPPER

Like most Cornish folk it seems that the Harveys, when they moved, seldom travelled far from family, friends and familiar surroundings. Until driven out of Cornwall by the cataclysm that befell mining in the final years of the 19th century when their main source of income was removed, most of the family stayed in the area of St Agnes, Truro and Redruth and so were at the centre of Cornwall's mining industry during its heyday. When the pedigree first picks them up in 1710 it looks as if Samuel(i) Harvey was living at St Agnes where he was married and his children were christened. St Agnes is a mining village on the rocky north coast where its great granite cliffs are pounded by Atlantic rollers. There has been mining at St Agnes since ancient times; archaeologists say copper was probably extracted there back in the Bronze Age. Indeed it would be surprising if primitive man had not noticed the copper lodes which can still be seen in those cliffs.

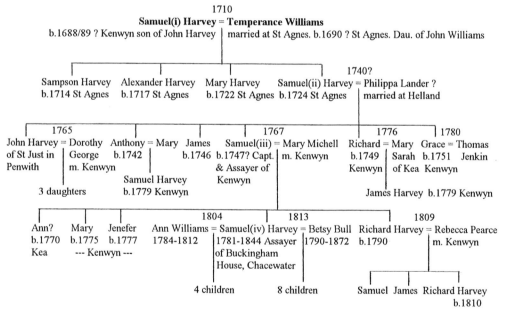

The Harveys of Chacewater - The early pedigree
Connects with the chart at page 33

Although there is some uncertainty about the composition of the second generation, it appears that Samuel's son, Samuel(ii) Harvey, had by about 1740 moved a few miles south from St Agnes to the large parish of Kenwyn near the city of Truro. Forty years on when Samuel(iv) was born, we find the family settled at the far west end of the parish in the village of Chacewater near one of the principal mines of the area. There in the next century the Harveys flourished and built two substantial houses which remain there today. They are just a short walk from what are now the ruins of Wheal Busy and four smaller mines, Creegbrauze, Wheal Daniell, Wheal Unity and Killifreath, upon which their livelihoods once depended. The last of the family to live in the village was Milly (Harriet Amelia) Harvey, a school teacher, who died there in 1944 aged a hundred. She was in her twenties when Wheal Busy started to run down. After working intermittently it closed finally in 1920.

The ruins of the principal engine house of Wheal Busy (Harvey's Shaft) at Chacewater. It was built in the 1850s and contained at different periods 80, 90 and 85 inch engines. (Photo: DB Barton c.1960s, Royal Cornwall Museum).

The story of this family's fortunes roughly tracks events in Cornish copper mining in which for at least a hundred years many of the Harvey menfolk were engaged as 'assayers'[1]. There was a resurgence in the industry in the early 1700s when two of the richest copper mines were at Chacewater and nearby North Downs. They were the first copper mines to bring in the new

---

[1] Assayers: Mining company employees or public servants who were responsible for taking and analysing samples of the ore to establish quality and price. See "Mining Talk" at the end of this Chapter (page 20).

steam-powered pumping engines in 1725/26. Towards the end of the century overproduction by new opencast mines in Anglesey caused a slump and in 1788 North Downs closed and even Chacewater and several other mines were idle for a time.

With the 1800s came rapid expansion; the Anglesey copper was worked out, the Napoleonic wars had increased demand, more efficient engines became available, water drainage improved, and the first seven miles of tracks for horse-drawn trams were laid in 1807. The trams took coal in and the ore back for smelting in Wales and went from Portreath on the coast past Chacewater, the mine later known as Wheal Busy and employing 700 men, to the large Poldice tin mine in Gwennap with 1200 miners. This was the most productive period of Cornish mining ever and for a time Cornwall again became the principal copper producer in the world.

It was during these boom years that mining really altered the landscape. Workers flocked into mining parishes: Camborne, Chacewater, Gwennap, St Day and other villages around Redruth all became thriving centres of industry with hundreds working underground, and hundreds more, including women and children, at the surface dressing the ore. It is difficult to imagine the harsh conditions that miners then had to suffer. As the mines deepened they had to cope with worsening ventilation and temperatures that could rise above 100 degrees F. Some miners faced long climbs down near vertical ladders to reach pitches more than 1500 feet below the surface. This sort of work could be done only by young men; mostly they were aged between 15 and 25. It was a dangerous trade: in Gwennap in the 1840s one in five men employed underground died violent deaths. Few miners lived much beyond 40.

Even at the surface conditions were uncomfortable. "The noise from the engines, from the dressing floors and the smell of arsenic and sulphur fumes filled the air, and the rivers were heavily polluted"- like a scene from Dante's Inferno! It was little better when the miners went home after an 8-10 hour shift. They lived in small, damp, overcrowded hovels of cob and thatch, generally built by themselves, which had mushroomed throughout mining districts; their few leisure hours were occupied with such brutish pastimes as cock-fighting, wrestling, bull-baiting and sometimes the grim business of wrecking.[2] Like fishermen and

---

[2] Wrecking was at one end the spontaneous scavenging of a wreck by a local community, and at the other it was organised bands luring a ship onto rocks, plundering its cargo and even drowning survivors. Wrecking was not as widespread as smuggling which during the 19th century became accepted practice by almost all sections of Cornish society from the humble tinner down on his luck, to the squire who liked his brandy, and his lady who dressed in lace.

Miners, 1900 feet down Dolcoath mine, climbing up to "grass". They just had their daily issue of tallow candles to work by and the brief illumination for this photograph would have been the only time these men saw anything beyond their immediate vicinity. Indeed some used to save their candles by climbing in the glimmer of their neighbour's so that they could use them at home. (Photo: JC Burrow c.1893, Royal Cornwall Museum).

farmworkers the miners found solace in drinking beer or smuggled spirits; Chacewater, which today has three pubs, then had about fifteen! Many of these were simple "Ale Houses" found on the outskirts of the village on lanes leading to nearby mines.

> Come all good Cornish boys walk in;
> Here's brandy, rum and shrub and gin;
> You can't do less than drink success
> To copper, fish and tin.   (From a 19th century pub sign)

Fortunate indeed were the assayers and other mining professionals not tied to the exhausting daily grind of the miner at the face. When King Copper effectively transformed Cornwall into an important component of the Industrial Revolution, many fortunes were made, but it was generally not the lowly miner who benefited. One exception was the famous Williams family of Gwennap and Scorrier. Originally humble tinners in Stithians, they became agents and managers for several local mine owners and by 1800 the family were controlling or managing a quarter of all the copper mines in Cornwall. It was John Williams, "the most dynamic and experienced of mine managers", who with William Lemon from 1748 began to drive forward the Great County Adit, an ambitious drainage scheme covering five parishes. It eventually succeeded in extending the life of as many as fifty mines well into the following century. Could this be the same Williams family into which Samuel(i) Harvey married at St Agnes in 1710 when he wed John William's daughter Temperance? If so, it was a fortuitous match which may have helped Samuel's grandson, Samuel(iii) Harvey, rise to become both a mine captain and assayer.

The mining boom reached its peak in the 1850s, but from about 1865 came the rapid collapse of first copper and then the tin market swamped by over-production abroad. It caused terrible destitution in Cornwall where by 1880 the number of miners had decreased by two thirds. Chacewater like other mining parishes became "depopulated and half derelict". Those of the "Cousin Jacks" who were young and fit enough took their skills to other continents - to the mines of North and South America, South Africa and Australia where some of their descendants live today.

These events of course influenced the younger generation of Harveys then living at Chacewater. Frederick Osmond Harvey and William Pellew Harvey were cousins who had trained as mining engineers. With the lack of prospects in Cornwall Frederick went as a mine manager to Portugal in 1885, and eight years later to a gold mine in Colorado; while William travelled to British Columbia in about 1890 where ten years later he was instrumental in establishing the first

Dominion Assay Office in Canada. Neither of the cousins returned to live in Cornwall. They met again at the Chicago World Fair in 1893 and a few years later each set up his own Mining Consultancy in London (Their stories are told in Chapter 5).

Scattered across the landscape of much of west Cornwall today are derelict engine houses with the arid spill of tunnelling waste spread around them in gorse covered heaps. They are virtually all that is now visible of this once flourishing industry. These massive stone structures, some as at Wheal Busy complete with chimney stack and boiler house, contained the huge beam engines, with cylinders up to 90 inches in diameter, which powered the mines - principally to drain them of water. They stand like giant tombstones, melancholy memorials to Cornwall's great mining tradition and to "the old men" of past generations whose arduous labour in the face of danger and privation brought prosperity to Cornwall for nearly two centuries.

St Agnes. Timbermen working at the Blue Hills mine at the 400 foot level. St Agnes lodes tended to be almost horizontal as here; the walls were generally sound, but when the ore was rich few rock pillars were left and a large number of wooden props were needed. (Photo: JC Burrows 1893, Royal Cornwall Museum).

Mining Talk

Adit - A tunnel through which water is drained out of a mine. See reference at page 17 to the benefits of the Great County Adit.

Assayer or **Assay Master** - A mining company employee or public servant who is responsible for taking and analysing samples of ore to establish quality and price. The two titles are synonymous. 'Assay Master', the older term, goes back to 1688 when it was used to describe the official of the Stannary Court who was in charge of tin metal at coinage, and one of whose functions was to strike a corner off each tin ingot to ensure that it was of acceptable quality. It was later (1825) used to describe a senior or consultant assayer, and then to mean a professional assayer who worked for several mines or for the public. On tin mines he is today known as the Sampler.

Captain - An honorary title given to managers, and in larger mines also to agents (under-managers) of mines. There are numerous varieties of Captain. It is thought to have been adopted in Elizabeth I's reign when German mining engineers came to England.

Lode - A deposit or vein of metallic ore occurring between definite limits in the surrounding rock.

Mine - A hole in the ground with a Cornishman at the bottom (old Cornish saying).

Opencast - Mining by excavating shallow ore from the surface. After a discovery at Anglesey in 1768, two opencast copper mines were able to flood the market to the great disadvantage of Cornish mines. The metal prices remained low until the 1790s when the Anglesey mines began to be worked out.

Purser - Mine company secretary

Stannaries - Mining districts of Cornwall and Devon under the jurisdiction of a Stannary Court determining tin mining issues.

Smelting - The process of extracting metal from an ore by heating. The lack of its own indigenous coal meant that Cornish copper smelting, which needed large quantities of coal, was generally done in south Wales. Tin, needing less coal, continued to be smelted in Cornwall until the tin mines finally closed.

Streaming - The old method of obtaining the ore from alluvial deposits washed into streams. Streaming rather than underground mining was the main source of Cornish tin at least until the middle of the 16th century.

Tinner - Anyone, miner, shareholder, merchant, mineral lord etc, who is involved with tin mining. A mineral lord owns the minerals under a piece of ground but is not necessarily the owner of the surface.

Wheal - The Cornish word for 'work', and hence 'a mine-working'.

East Pool mine at Illogan 1080 foot down. A typical scene on a main ladderway, as men are coming up from below and climbing on upwards towards the next level, passing two timbermen. Ladders were once the only way to the surface. Two tallow candles are hanging from the bearded timberman's shirt.
(Photo: JC Burrow 1893, Royal Cornwall Museum).

Chapter 3

HEREDITY AND THE FUTURE

There is no cell in our bodies that has not been transmitted to us by our ancestors. Colour of eyes, type of skin, the shape of our nose, in fact our whole appearance, our gestures and personality, the depth of emotions, sense of humour and our small talents, all these are determined by our genes at conception. We possess minds, bodies and feelings bequeathed to us by people, most of them long since dead, who have made us what we are - or at least what we started out in life with.

In a way longevity is also inherited. It is genes that mostly determine our physical weaknesses and vulnerability to certain diseases and they will therefore often affect when we will die and from what cause. Doctors say that "two thirds of people alive today will die as a result of their genes and not from the specific effect of diseases". In this genetic battle the influence of medical treatment, on which we now spend so much, is puny; or as the American physician Oliver Wendell Holmes said, "if all the medicines ever prescribed had been thrown into the sea, it would have been better for mankind but worse for the fish".

Our current efforts to "improve" the genes of humans, animals and vegetables to give us some short term "benefits" - a longer healthier life, leaner meat, durable tomatoes - are worrying. The implications for future generations of such perverse genetic tampering are unexplored. We do know that the alterations to genetic patterns that result from inbreeding, once common in small Cornish communities and referred to later, tend to increase their vulnerability to disease and hence affect longevity. It may therefore be reassuring for the Harvey family to know that, based on data from five generations of ancestors, their average life expectancy handsomely exceeds three score years and ten. This ignores several premature deaths, one in Africa, it is said from alcohol abuse, one at the hands of South American Indians and other similar misadventures.

Difficult though it is to distinguish between the influences of heredity and environment, there is strong evidence of a genetic element in the predisposition of some families towards following certain occupations or natural skills. This can persist for generations, as it did with the Harveys, father and son, who continued for years in the meticulous and precise work of the mineral assayer. But then along comes some strong but divergent genetic strain producing a volatile mixture of talent and outlook, not easy for the family to assimilate. Such was the experience of one Harvey father, an assiduous, painstaking and highly successful assayer, who found that the heir to his business was a very unworldly artistic and rather indolent son for whom any form of commerce was anathema!

The geographical position of Cornwall has led to its comparative isolation over the centuries, giving it a history separate from that of England and its own distinctive language, a variant of the Celtic tongue which was in common use in the County right up to the 18th century. One effect of this isolation, compounded by the fairly static nature of the old close-knit mining and fishing communities, has been to increase marriage within families - Cousin Jack with Cousin Jenny. This is evident in the large numbers who share the old Cornish family names - Penrose, Couch, Bray, Pascoe, Polkinghorne, Truscott, Trefusis, Hosken, Davey, Moyle and the rest. Except for their immediate family, surprisingly few of them are aware of their relationship to others who bear their name. Yet it is clear from our research into such families as Penrose, Hichens and Pellew, that those with the same Cornish name are almost all related, some confusingly often, and that most of these forgotten family links are no more than three generations back.

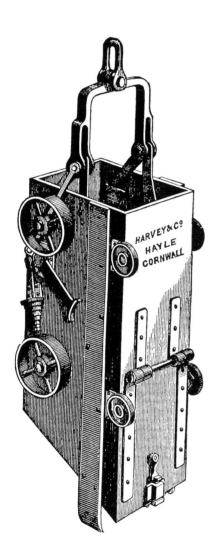

The same sort of amnesia probably applies in the case of Harvey, a name which originated from Brittany and is widespread in Cornwall. This may be why we have so far failed to find any link between the Harveys of Chacewater and other Harvey families. The best known of that name in the mining business was John Harvey who in 1770 started the great Harvey Foundry at Hayle where, for the next century and more, some of the giant engines on

From an advertisement by the Harvey Foundry which sold mining equipment all over the world

which the industry depended were built. Richard Trevithick, the famous Cornish engineer and inventor, who married John Harvey's daughter Jane in 1797, was the first to put a high pressure steam locomotive (with a Harvey boiler) onto rails - 21 years before his friend George Stephenson with his "Rocket".

A window in Truro Cathedral commemorates a family with so many similarities to the Harveys of Chacewater that a connection must surely exist. It is a sad story. The family is that of Samuel Harvey 1819-99 whose wife Emma and seven of their children predeceased him. All seven, who are named, died in their twenties. As in the Chacewater family, the eldest son was christened Samuel after his father at Kenwyn in 1846, but he was drowned aged only 20. The family may be descended from Samuel(ii)'s son Anthony who had a son, Samuel, in 1779.

Truro Cathedral was built between 1880-1910 on the site of the 13th century St Mary's church where the following served as rectors, William W Harvey 1839-60, Edmund G Harvey 1860-65 and Clement Fox Harvey 1875-85. In contrast no family has so far claimed the notorious Cornish criminal known in the French and English press of 1905 only as "the Anarchist Harvey". In Paris that year he threw a bomb at Alfonso, the young King of Spain, while he was on a state visit. The King was unhurt but it killed a horse and injured fifteen people.

The Royal Cornwall Gazette reported that "the Anarchist Harvey" came from "a well known and respected Cornish family". Although he has never been further identified, the Chacewater Harveys have suffered by association. The following year, 1906, another bomb was thrown at King Alfonso, this time during his wedding in Madrid. The police immediately arrested 20 year old Dick Harvey, one of the Chacewater family who was then working in Seville, mistaking him for his notorious namesake. After interrogation Dick was eventually released, ruffled and very indignant.

Claughton Pellew Harvey aged about 20
(Photo: Anne Tennent)

As far as we know, all the long-lived Harveys of Chacewater died or left Cornwall more than fifty years ago with the last to be born there being the artist Claughton Pellew Harvey in 1890. He and his younger brother, Edward who was born in London after the family returned from Canada, were Cornish on both sides going back as many generations as records have survived. Claughton and his parents left the land of their birth at a time of great upheaval as mining in Cornwall had gone into terminal decline. Even smuggling was no longer so profitable! The new china clay and tourist industries had hardly begun to offset the worst economic effects of the slump, but it was the impact of the direct rail link to London that quickly spawned new business and gave hope. It used to take all of forty uncomfortable hours to reach Falmouth from London by stagecoach. That was before 1859 when Brunel built his bridge over the river Tamar, the border with England, allowing trains into the County. But the railway not only brought visitors; on the return journey to London the trains began to take back Cornish produce, such as mackerel caught by the Mount's Bay drifters, early broccoli and potatoes. Spring flowers and other exports followed and Cornwall soon found itself with a thriving horticultural industry.

Our century has seen the building of a large road bridge over the Tamar and now great highways for the car are reaching right to the heart of Cornwall where tourism is predominant. Twenty three years ago the Cornish writer, Nigel Tangye, believed that this was one of the few areas of England that still retained its "intrinsic individuality created by centuries of history", and that Cornwall was "still mainly populated by Cornishmen, although every year further dilution occurs". Today better access has brought a huge invasion of visitors and especially new residents, mostly of retirement age; yet at the same time Cornwall is losing its young who see better prospects elsewhere. It cannot be long before the distinctive character of this ancient land and its people is swamped by this 'foreign' invasion, far more insidious than those of the past mounted by the Spanish or French.

Before this happens it would be wise for the expatriate descendants of those such as the Harveys, who take pride in their Cornish ancestry, to go and see this "enchanted" corner of England for themselves. It has been the home of the Harveys' Celtic forebears for centuries, probably ever since they arrived from Brittany. The dramatic beauty of Cornwall's granite cliffs, its barren moorland and the lushness of its wooded valleys may be almost timeless; but if they delay their visit, it may be too late to meet a true Cornishman. The strong, stoical and stubbornly independent men and women who made this a place apart will be no more.

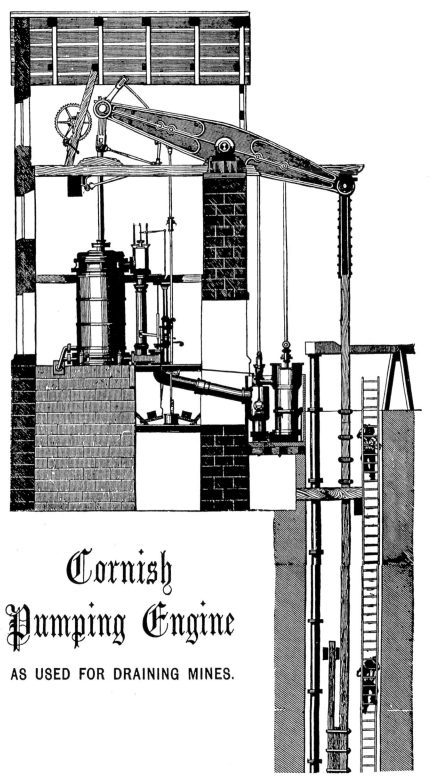

Cornish Pumping Engine

AS USED FOR DRAINING MINES.

A cross-section through an Engine House and upper shaft from an 1884 advertisement for Harvey's Foundry at Hayle (Royal Cornwall Museum).

PART 2

FAMILY TALES

-o-o-o-o-o-o-o-

The past is a foreign country: they do things differently there

LP Hartley ('The Go-Between' 1953)

The entrance to St Paul's Church, Chacewater, built in 1828 when it was consecrated as a Chapel-of-Ease until Chacewater became a separate Parish in 1837. Many of the Harvey family lie in the graveyard. The church has the 'Harvey window' (illustrated on the back cover) which was donated by Charles Harvey 1838-1930 and his siblings in memory of their parents, Richard and Sophia Harvey who lived at Buckingham House on the Terrace at Chacewater (See the Chart on page 40). Richard and Sophia's grave is beneath the yew tree on the left of the picture.

Chapter 4

HARVEY OF CHACEWATER

The Harvey name comes from Brittany. It derives from the Old Breton 'Haervin', literally meaning battle or carnage-worthy. Original bearers of the name were perhaps soldiers or had soldierly qualities; or could it have been a term of disparagement - 'cannon fodder!' In Scotland the name is spelt Harvie, while the English version, Harvey or occasionally Hervey, is most common in Cornwall and south Devon as well as in Staffordshire and East Anglia. The name is said to have been introduced by Breton followers of William the Conqueror in the Old French form of 'Hervé'.

Direct links between Cornwall and Brittany go back long before King William landed at Pevensey. After all, these two Celtic races, each facing out into the Atlantic less than 100 sea miles apart and blown by the same gales, share a common ancestry. It goes back at least to the 5th and 6th centuries when many Gaelic speaking Britons settled in Brittany such that the Province became known as Britannia Minor, giving rise to its present name. Two districts of Brittany were once called Cornwall ('Cornouailles') and Devon ('Domnonée') until the names were lost when both were combined into Penthièvre. Then there were the famous Breton 'saints', mentioned earlier, who came over to strengthen their Cornish brothers against the heathen English. The close ties that have existed between these two races leave little doubt that this Harvey family were true Cornish Celts stiffened by some belligerent Breton blood.

In more recent times it has been the fortunes of Cornish mining that have determined those of the Harveys of Chacewater. When they first appear in records it seems that the family were living on the north coast at St Agnes where on 15th April 1710 Samuel(i) Harvey married Temperance Williams. The great expansion in copper mining was just beginning, and this may be why their son, Samuel(ii), at about the time of his marriage in 1740, moved inland to the parish of Kenwyn to be at the heart of this booming industry where no doubt other members of the family were already working. It was then we think Samuel and his new wife settled in the village of Chacewater, on the turnpike road between Truro and Redruth, which was to be the Harvey family home for the next two hundred years.

Apart from the long association with Chacewater and the mining industry, a feature of this family is that they descend through five generations of Samuels - and hence the need to number them. I thought this distinctive until we discovered that, while our Samuel(iv) in Chacewater was fathering a handsomely large family, there were two other Samuel Harveys with families elsewhere in Kenwyn parish. As explained in Chapter 3, these other Harveys would probably be 'cousins' of Samuel(iv), and one may even have been his first cousin, a Samuel baptised in 1779, the son of his uncle Anthony Harvey.

Chacewater today is a quiet village deserted by the main road which runs a mile or so to the north. Its houses are spread about over a wide area of broken undulating ground and small hills which overlook the village centre. The name used to be spelt Chase-water meaning a hunting ground by a river. The river is the Carnon which rises in the surrounding hills and runs as a stream through the village, flowing out into the Fal estuary (Carrick Roads) seven miles to the south. Chacewater, which was a distant part of the parish of Kenwyn, five miles away, became a separate parish in 1837 with its own church, St Paul's, overlooking the village on the southern side. There is some terracing, a characteristic of many old mining villages like St Day, Four Lanes, and Lanner. Hundreds of miners' hovels must once have covered every piece of level ground around the village and the five mines that lay within a mile of it.

The principal 'Chacewater' mine came to be called 'Wheal Busy' and by 1865 'Great Wheal Busy', whose main shaft was named "Harvey's shaft" - possibly after Samuel(iii) Harvey who, besides being an assayer, was mine captain there. He built a house on land, later known as The Terrace, leased from Lord Falmouth (the Boscawen family) who owned most of the village. A well worn miner's path still runs from there through sandy hillocks and scrub to the ruins of Wheal Busy barely 600 yards away. The sound of its great 80 inch steam engine must have been a rhythmic accompaniment to family life on The Terrace.

Buckingham House, Chacewater, built by the Harveys before 1840, continued to be the family home for the next hundred years. It is now divided into Latchets and Little Latchets (Photo c.1930, Richard F Harvey).

In the 1841 census Samuel(iv), an assayer like his father and purser for the Wheal Tehidy tin mine at Redruth, can be seen as a man of substance. He and his second wife, Elizabeth (Betsy) Bull, and five of his twelve children were living with two servants at Buckingham House, and he was leasing five acres of land near the church as well as an Assay Office at the back of the market. Some years later the family built a second house on the Terrace around an original two-roomed cottage and this became the home of Samuel(v)'s widow Philippa Grace Pellew, the daughter of another Wheal Busy mine captain, and their two young sons. They called it Exmouth House because of Philippa's connection with the family of the late Edward Pellew, Lord Exmouth, who was a national hero of the time, second only to Nelson (See Chapter 6).

Exmouth House, Chacewater (1997), built by the Harveys about 1870. Philippa Harvey née Pellew, who named the house after the late Admiral, lived here after her husband's death and it eventually became the home of her grandchildren.

When he died in 1844, Samuel(iv) and his family had become influential in the life of the village and its mining community. His eldest son, Samuel(v) had taken over his assaying business and replaced him as purser of Tehidy. Richard his second son, whose mother, Ann Williams, had died when he was born, was running a combined grocers and post office in Fore Street by the Market Place, and later moved into Buckingham House. His third son, William Bull Harvey, ran a drapers store also in Fore Street and leased the Assay Office nearby, while his son-in-law William Sims, married to his eldest daughter Elizabeth, was the innkeeper of the Red Lion. The inn still stands but has a modern name, The Rambling Miner - an oddity in a County where miners are an extinct species.

The size of Samuel(iv)'s family of 12 children was not untypical (See chart opposite). It reflected the confidence of the years following Trafalgar and Waterloo, the accession of the young Queen Victoria and not least Samuel's own increasing prosperity as copper mining started to boom again. His children too were fruitful and he eventually accumulated no less than 63 grandchildren - quite a dynasty! Unfortunately their impact was short-lived. It was mainly these grandchildren that, in the last three decades of the century, were to feel the effects of the mining slump that destroyed the industry and with it their prospects for working in Cornwall.

The collapse of Cornwall's copper and tin markets began around 1865. Thereafter not many, apart from the older members of the family, were able to remain in Cornwall. While a few survived there well into the 20th century, the rest had left to seek fortunes elsewhere taking their mining and other skills and traditions with them. They seem to have spread out like thistledown on the wind - not only to other parts of England and Wales, but to the mining areas of Portugal, the USA, Canada, Australia and elsewhere.

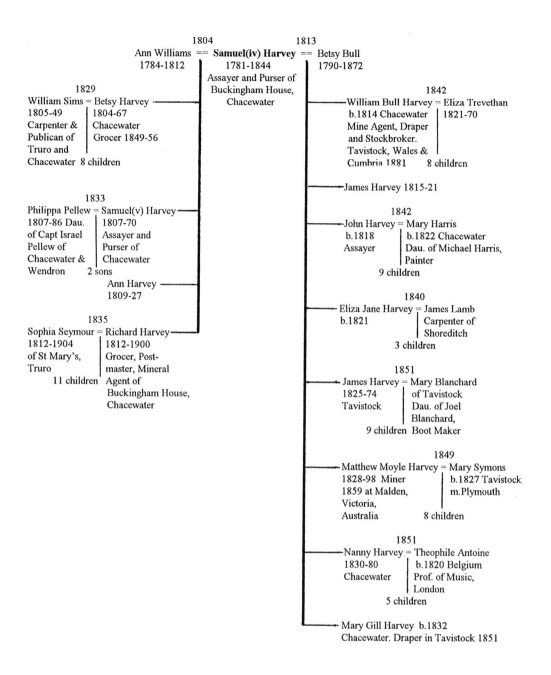

1804   1813
Ann Williams == **Samuel(iv) Harvey** == Betsy Bull
1784-1812   1781-1844   1790-1872
Assayer and Purser of
Buckingham House,
Chacewater

1829
William Sims = Betsy Harvey
1805-49   1804-67
Carpenter &   Chacewater
Publican of   Grocer 1849-56
Truro and
Chacewater   8 children

1833
Philippa Pellew = Samuel(v) Harvey
1807-86 Dau.   1807-70
of Capt Israel   Assayer and
Pellew of   Purser of
Chacewater &   Chacewater
Wendron   2 sons

Ann Harvey
1809-27

1835
Sophia Seymour = Richard Harvey
1812-1904   1812-1900
of St Mary's,   Grocer, Post-
Truro   master, Mineral
11 children   Agent of
Buckingham House,
Chacewater

1842
William Bull Harvey = Eliza Trevethan
b.1814 Chacewater   1821-70
Mine Agent, Draper
and Stockbroker.
Tavistock, Wales &
Cumbria 1881   8 children

James Harvey 1815-21

1842
John Harvey = Mary Harris
b.1818   b.1822 Chacewater
Assayer   Dau. of Michael Harris,
Painter
9 children

1840
Eliza Jane Harvey = James Lamb
b.1821   Carpenter of
Shoreditch
3 children

1851
James Harvey = Mary Blanchard
1825-74   of Tavistock
Tavistock   Dau. of Joel
Blanchard,
9 children   Boot Maker

1849
Matthew Moyle Harvey = Mary Symons
1828-98 Miner   b.1827 Tavistock
1859 at Malden,   m.Plymouth
Victoria,
Australia   8 children

1851
Nanny Harvey = Theophile Antoine
1830-80   b.1820 Belgium
Chacewater   Prof. of Music,
London
5 children

Mary Gill Harvey b.1832
Chacewater. Draper in Tavistock 1851

The twelve children of Samuel(iv) Harvey who gave him 63 grandchildren
This chart follows on from the early pedigree shown on page 13. More details of some of Samuel(iv)'s grandchildren, who are only numbered above, can be found in each of the four charts in Chapter 5, pages 35, 36, 40, 43.

Chapter 5

THISTLEDOWN ON THE WIND

These are stories of what happened to some of the children and grandchildren of Samuel(iv) Harvey when they left Cornwall and where they and their offspring went. After centuries of stability, the loss of prospects in what had once been their homeland turned some of them into notable travellers. They took their expertise and traditions all over the world and a few made international reputations in the process. The Harveys were just a small part of the great Cornish exodus that occurred when the copper and tin ran out (Readers may find it useful to refer to the sketch pedigrees on the previous page and in this chapter to identify the various individuals and branches of this large family that are mentioned)

Wales, Cumbria, London, Paris and the World
Descendants of Samuel(iv) and Betsy Bull

Some of the Chacewater Harveys did not travel far. As early as 1848 William Bull Harvey, Betsy Bull's eldest son, had moved his increasing family just over the river Tamar to Tavistock where three of his sons found work in the copper mine. He was joined there by his two brothers, James and Matthew Moyle Harvey. By 1871 events had made William Bull with most of his now grown-up family leave Tavistock for Wales where his father-in-law had made his home twenty years before. They settled for a few years at Aberystwyth on Cardigan Bay where his son Richard became the manager of the Dyffryn Castell Hotel but died of bronchitis - a result of mining at Tavistock from the age of 15.

Meanwhile his father had moved on to find better prospects in the industrial north of England, and in the 1881 census we find three generations of William Bull's family settled at Barrow-in-Furness in Cumbria. While his brother James and his nine children had remained to eke out a living in Tavistock, Matthew Moyle Harvey took his young family to Australia together with his 18 year old nephew Henry Harvey (eldest son of Richard and Sophia of Buckingham House) where they worked in the mines around Malden in Victoria. Sadly Henry died there of dysentery, but Matthew flourished and a descendant of his, Harvey Bell, is today the Shire Engineer of Junee in New South Wales.

William Bull Harvey's other brother, John the assayer with his wife Mary Harris (Chart below) remained behind in Cornwall. However when Brunel bridged the Tamar in 1859 and opened Cornwall up to the outside world, their son James found work with the new Great Western Railway. He settled in London and it was his son, Frederick Hubert Harvey, who in 1912 founded the famous Harvey School in Paris. See "A Musical Lady" in the Supplement (page 70).

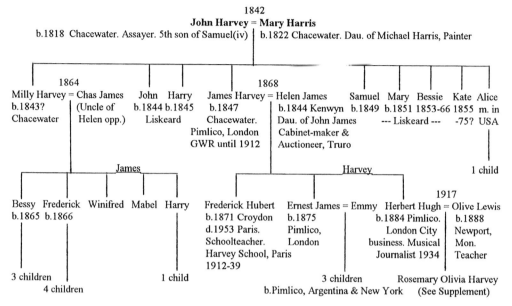

Children and grandchildren of John Harvey & Mary Harris
Connects with the chart on pages 33

The Mountains of BC and Back
Descendants of Samuel(v) and Philippa Pellew

Samuel(v) and Philippa's two sons, Harvey Pellew Harvey and William Henry Harvey were both assayers in their father's business in Chacewater. The slump had already begun to affect them by the time Samuel died in 1870. His sons were only in their early 30s but they stayed nevertheless, although Harvey Pellew, the elder brother who remained a bachelor until he was 52, later moved up the road to Truro where the family owned properties in Richmond Hill. To this day their descendants continue to receive peppercorn ground rents for houses on the Hill. The younger brother, William Henry, his wife Emma Moyle and their children moved into Exmouth House in about 1886. He is remembered for the fine sight he made when driving out with his Dalmatian carriage dogs of which he was overtly fond. On the other hand it is said that he was extremely strict with his two daughters. Emma Florence (Aunt Flo) never married and was still living in Exmouth House in 1902 after the deaths of her father and his brother, while Ettie had eloped with the groom, Frank Yeo, and went to live in Gloucestershire. Ettie's daughter, Winnie, emigrated to Australia where her son, Malcolm Bryant, still lives.

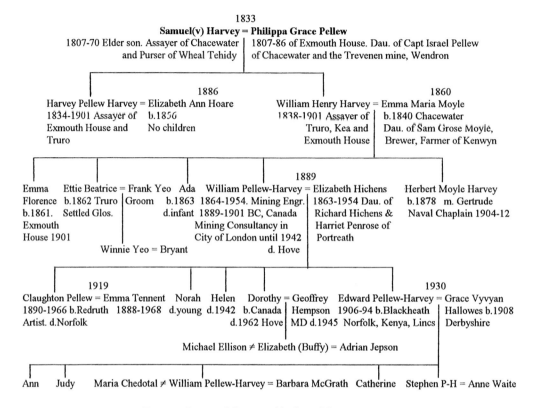

1833
Samuel(v) Harvey = Philippa Grace Pellew
1807-70 Elder son. Assayer of Chacewater | 1807-86 of Exmouth House. Dau. of Capt Israel Pellew
and Purser of Wheal Tehidy | of Chacewater and the Trevenen mine, Wendron

1886 | **1860**
Harvey Pellew Harvey = Elizabeth Ann Hoare | William Henry Harvey = Emma Maria Moyle
1834-1901 Assayer of   b.1856 | 1838-1901 Assayer of   b.1840 Chacewater
Exmouth House and   No children | Truro, Kea and   Dau. of Sam Grose Moyle,
Truro | Exmouth House   Brewer, Farmer of Kenwyn

1889
Emma   Ettie Beatrice = Frank Yeo   Ada   William Pellew-Harvey = Elizabeth Hichens   Herbert Moyle Harvey
Florence   b.1862 Truro   Groom   b.1863   1864-1954. Mining Engr.   1863-1954 Dau. of   b.1878 m. Gertrude
b.1861.   Settled Glos.   d.infant   1889-1901 BC, Canada   Richard Hichens &   Naval Chaplain 1904-12
Exmouth   Mining Consultancy in   Harriet Penrose of
House 1901   City of London until 1942   Portreath
Winnie Yeo = Bryant   d. Hove

1919 | **1930**
Claughton Pellew = Emma Tennent   Norah   Helen   Dorothy = Geoffrey   Edward Pellew-Harvey = Grace Vyvyan
1890-1966 b.Redruth   1888-1968   d.young   d.1942   b.Canada | Hempson   1906-94 b.Blackheath | Hallowes b.1908
Artist. d.Norfolk   d.1962 Hove | MD d.1945   Norfolk, Kenya, Lincs | Derbyshire

Michael Ellison ≠ Elizabeth (Buffy) = Adrian Jepson

Ann   Judy   Maria Chedotal ≠ William Pellew-Harvey = Barbara McGrath   Catherine   Stephen P-H = Anne Waite

Descendants of Samuel(v) & Philippa Pellew

Connects with the earlier chart on page 33, is continued in the page 77 chart and links into the Pellew chart on page 47

William the Wanderer

Emma and Ettie had two brothers. The elder, William Pellew Harvey, left Truro Grammar School at 16, served an apprenticeship in mine engineering at Swansea for three years and then worked for John F Penrose & Sons at Redruth. Aged 25 he married Elizabeth Hichens, the niece of John Farran Penrose, his boss, and they emigrated with their baby son, Claughton, to work in the gold mine at Golden near the source of the great Columbia river, high up in the Rocky Mountains of British Columbia. From here he was also able to visit mining areas in Ontario and Nova Scotia. Four years later he set up an Assay Office in Vancouver and when he left to return to London in 1901, such was the reputation he had made in the industry, it had become the Dominion Assay Office for the whole of Canada. By then William had hyphenated his name in the fashion of the time and had become distinctively 'Pellew-Harvey'. In London he established a mining consultancy in the City for which he worked for the next 40 years, travelling all over the globe.

William Pellew-Harvey 1864-1954
President of the Institution of Mining and Metalurgy 1931 (Photo: Liz Addie).

Thanks to his mother Emma's eye for publicity a report of William's departures overseas frequently appeared in the papers. Russia, where at one time he represented the Rio Tinto Company, was a frequent destination. A report he wrote in 1905 for the Spassky Company was instrumental in the development of the copper reserves in an area of over 100 square miles around Akmolinsk in south-west Siberia. His was a hardy life; during the Russian revolution of 1917 he escaped unharmed when the train he was on was attacked, and in the wilds of Magyar (Hungary) he had out of courtesy to eat his host's local delicacy, sheep's eyeballs. He was several times in Australia visiting mines in Victoria and working in association with Consolidated Mines of New South Wales at Cobar.

In 1931 William received the industry's final accolade when he became President of the Institution of Mining & Metallurgy of which he had then been a member for thirty years. His cousin, Dick Harvey, joined his partnership in 1933 and for four years travelled for them in Africa and South America. When war came in 1939 the assiduous William at the age of 75 was still going to his office in the City each day even when bombs were falling. He finally retired three years later, his only disappointment being that neither of his sons had followed him into the business on which he had lavished so much of his life and energy. He died at 90 within three days of his wife, Elizabeth, to whom he had been married for 64 years. The Supplement has details of some of their descendants among whom a grandson, 'The Trader' (page 77), seems to have inherited his grandfather's thirst for travel to remote and distant places.

Claughton the Artist

Meanwhile Claughton, William's sensitive elder son of whom he had once despaired, achieved a measure of success on his own terms. He had been a pacifist during the First World War and had suffered accordingly. Afterwards he had gained a national reputation as an artist of the countryside, with the twin themes of peace and tradition. This was all despite a severe handicap - his aversion to modern commerce and publicity which were so much part of his father's life. Perhaps it was to assert his individuality that he dropped the Harvey from his surname and signed his pictures simply as Claughton Pellew. See the Supplement - "A Shy Cornishman" (page 63).

The Battleship HMS Victorious (12,350 tons) in which Herbert Moyle Harvey served as Chaplain 1907-8. Launched in 1895 she had 4 x 12 inch guns and a complement of 672 (Photo: National Maritime Museum 1913).

Herbert the Sailor

William Pellew-Harvey had little in common with his younger brother, Herbert Moyle Harvey, who he said had "socialist tendencies" - not the first churchman to be accused of that! Herbert was the only one of the Chacewater family to follow the Pellew seafaring tradition. He spent eight years at sea as a Naval Chaplain serving in six different ships including in the battleship *HMS Victorious*.

Thereafter he was based in Devon and was for five years Chaplain of St Katherine's-upon-the-Hoe within The Royal Citadel at Plymouth. It was under the walls of The Citadel that Captain Edward Pellew RN had almost single-handedly saved the passengers from the wreck of the *Dutton* 125 years before (See page 46).

The Wild West & the Portuguese Line
Descendants of Richard Harvey and Sophia Seymour of Buckingham House

Richard Harvey 1812-1900, Grocer, Postmaster and Mineral Agent of Chacewater and his wife Sophia Seymour 1812-1904 (Photos: Richard F Harvey).

Charles the Adventurer

Samuel(v)'s younger brother, Richard and his wife Sophia raised eleven children in Chacewater. Henry, the eldest, as mentioned earlier, died aged 24 six years after he arrived in Australia. Charles, the second son, travelled widely and made his fortune in mining, finally returning to Chacewater in 1913 when he was in his 70s to live with some of his spinster sisters in the family home where he was born. He died there aged 91. His nephew, Dick Harvey, later remembered him as "a pioneer mining engineer of soldierly bearing, always well attired. He joined in the gold rushes in the western States of the USA and was quick on the draw and a good horseman. He acquired an alluvial gold property[3] in Colorado which worked for some years." Charles' final mining enterprise was to start the Carnon

---

[3] No evidence of this "alluvial gold property" in Colorado has been found.

Valley Tin Works processing alluvial ore dredged from the river flats four miles down stream from Chacewater. This continued for 16 years until his death in 1930. Charles had a generous and gregarious nature. He donated a beautiful stained glass window to St Paul's church in memory of his parents (pictured on the back cover), provided the village with a pavilion and other sports facilities on land given by Lord Falmouth, and, after a long-running disagreement with the vicar, gave him his car, a new two-seater Lagonda sports coupé, after the old man decided he had become a danger on the narrow Cornish roads.

Seven Sisters

Charles had seven sisters of whom only two, Fanny and Caroline, married and moved away. The others either remained at Chacewater or returned there from time to time. Sophia was a dressmaker and Milly and Helen taught at Green Bank, a private school for girls a few doors away from Buckingham House. Three of the sisters were over 90 when they died; the last of them, Milly, reached her century.

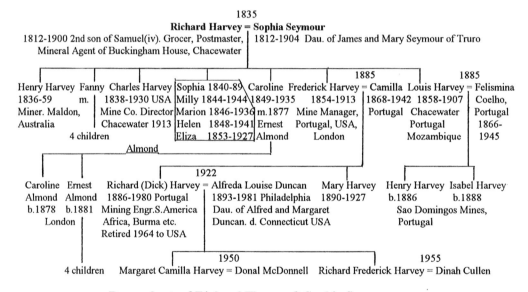

Descendants of Richard Harvey & Sophia Seymour
This chart follows from that on page 33 and is extended on page 73

Fred & Louis

Charles' two younger brothers, Frederick Osmond and Louis William Harvey, who were some twenty years his junior, found their way to southern Portugal where they worked for the Mason & Barry Mines at Sao Domingos near Mertola. There in 1885 they married Portuguese girls, Camilla and Felismina, who each bore a boy and a girl. Frederick who had previously visited mines in the USA and New Zealand, went in 1893 to take over as manager of the Twin Lakes Gold Mine in Colorado - 14,000 feet up in the Rockies. By 1902 he was back in London where, like his cousin William Pellew-Harvey, he established a mining partnership in the City. William had also been mining in the Rockies but a thousand miles to the north of him. Meanwhile little is known of Frederick's younger brother, Louis, who had probably remained in Portugal. A family story has it that he was the 'black sheep' and was 'sent to the colonies'. He died in Mozambique on the East African coast in 1907.

Richard the Rover

Frederick Harvey's son, Richard (known as Dick), was born in Portugal but educated in England at Shrewsbury School and at the Royal College of Science. He gained his mining certificates after working ninety shifts at the Carnbrae and Tincroft mines between Redruth and Camborne. In 1906 aged twenty he determined to gain more field experience and went to Seville in Spain. It was here that the police arrested him on suspicion of being "the Anarchist Harvey", but released him with apologies soon after. Further work followed at a large partly explored copper proposition in Chile (1907), as an assayer for the Cape Copper Company in Namaqualand, 300 miles north of Cape Town (1909), and as mining engineer for the Tavoy Tungsten Company in Burma (1913). Returning to England at the start of the Great War in 1914, Dick joined Mason & Barry Pyrites the following year as underground superintendent at Sao Domingos where his father and uncle Louis had once worked and he had been born. Four years later he was off to Mexico to work for Mazapil Copper, 100 miles south-west of Monterrey. It was on his return in some luxury on board the RMS Mauritania that Dick met his future wife, an American from Philadelphia, Alfreda Duncan (known as Teddy). Amongst the guests at their London wedding was his cousin William Pellew-Harvey with whom a decade later he was destined to work .

Dick's remarkably itinerant mining career continued with barely a pause. He spent five uncomfortable years working for Jantar Tin near Jos in central Nigeria living "in a pair of semi-detached mud huts". He and Teddy were back in England in 1926 coinciding with the General Strike. It was a case of all hands to the pump; Dick became an Auxiliary Policeman and his young cousin Edward Pellew-Harvey, William's younger son, drove a London bus throughout the strike. After Nigeria, Dick took Teddy and their children back to Portugal where he became a manager of Lagares Tin near Viseu in the north. Uncle Charles Harvey's death at Buckingham House in 1930 (from whom Dick, an executor, received a handsome legacy) and the slump that followed the Wall Street crash of the year before, caused their return to London. There in 1933 Dick joined his cousin William's City firm of mining consultants, and over the following four years undertook projects for them in the Gold Coast/Ghana, West Africa (1933-34), Southern Rhodesia/Zimbabwe (1935), Colombia (1935-36) and Egypt (1937). It is hard today to imagine what difficulties Dick must have faced on his journeys. To reach the Viborita Gold Mines at Amalfi in Colombia, he had to go by steamship to Jamaica, on a banana boat to Barranquilla on the coast, 400 miles by train to Medellin, and finally using mules over the 70 miles of mountain tracks to Amalfi on the Porce river.

Dick Harvey and Alfreda (Teddy) Duncan's wedding group, London 1922. On the bride's left is William Pellew-Harvey and beyond him the bride's sister, Margaret Carrington. (Photo: Richard F Harvey)

At the start of the Second World War in 1939 Dick, who had for 18 months been managing an insolvent Slate Quarry near Oporto for the Receivers, found himself stranded there with his family unable to return to England. Ships in the Bay of Biscay were being sunk by German U-boats, the German offensive against France was threatening, and General Franco had closed the frontiers of Spain while the Civil War there was being fought to a conclusion. Finally in February 1940 the family succeeded in crossing Spain like refugees in a sealed train, walked over the French frontier and after many tiring delays reached Calais, seething with soldiers and sailors, to board a grossly overloaded ferry. After dodging some floating mines on the crossing they arrived safely in London. The bombs came later. Despite pressure from Teddy's relatives for the family to join them in America "before Britain's certain defeat and occupation", the family remained in England. Indeed they stayed until 1964. In that year their son Richard emigrated to Australia and Dick and Teddy went to live near their daughter Margaret and her American husband Donal McDonnell in Connecticut. There, 16 years later, they died within eight months of each other; Dick was 94 and Teddy 87. See "The Submariner" in the Supplement (page 73).

Boot Maker to the Navy
William Sims and Elizabeth Williams Harvey of the Red Lion and their Descendants

Samuel(iv)'s eldest child was christened Elizabeth (Betsy) Williams Harvey in Kenwyn parish church in 1804. There, 25 years later, she married William Sims, a carpenter of Truro where in 1830-31 he became the landlord of the Daniell Arms in Lemon Street. When his father, John Sims, died (from inflammation of the liver!) in 1842, he took over the Red Lion in Chacewater from him until his own death seven years later. His widow then made a living by running a grocers in Higher Fore Street, Chacewater. Elizabeth and William had eight children of whom only three boys and two girls reached maturity. John, the eldest became a carpenter in Truro, and Josiah, the youngest, also a carpenter, married a London girl, Phillis Eaton, and moved to Camberwell where in 1898 their son, William James Sims founded a road haulage firm, WJ Sims Ltd, which is still in business. The middle son, William Harvey Sims born in Chacewater in 1836 married Jane Crossing, the daughter of a Devonport mason. William became a boot maker to the Navy with a shoe shop near Devonport naval dockyard. Malcolm Sims now living at Great Bookham, Surrey, is a descendant of William and Jane Sims of Devonport.

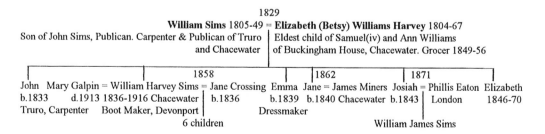

Descendants of William Sims & Elizabeth (Betsy) Williams Harvey
Connects with the chart on page 33

Captain Sir Edward Pellew RN 1757-1833, later Admiral Lord Exmouth, painted by Thomas Lawrence c.1799 (Photo: National Maritime Museum).

Chapter 6

THE SEAMEN
Pellew

When on a cold January day in 1833 Samuel(v) Harvey married Philippa Pellew at St Paul's, the new church on the hill overlooking Chacewater, quite a fresh dimension was added to the Harvey family. Although Philippa's father and brother, both named Israel, were mining Captains, the Pellews were by long tradition not miners but seafarers. Indeed on the very morning of Philippa's wedding she received the sad news of the death the previous day of one of the finest sailors of his generation - her cousin, Edward Pellew.

Edward was a distinguished member of another large Cornish family. Records show that the Pellews were settled in south-west Cornwall as early as the 14th century and remained for some 500 years in the area once known as the Hundred of Kerrier. This is the most southerly part of England and includes the barren Lizard peninsula, the old tin mining areas around Helston and Breage, the granite moorlands around Mabe, the little port of Penryn and the tidewater parishes of St Gluvias, Budock and Mylor. Tradition has it that the Pellews came originally from Normandy, landing at Pengersick Castle in Mounts Bay (behind Praa Sands). Until the 17th century the majority were established around Breage[4] where they owned land. Thereafter they moved east to Mabe and other parishes which gave access to the sheltered harbours of Falmouth and Penryn.

Edward Pellew was at least the fifth generation of the family that went to sea. He was just 13 when he joined his first ship, *Juno*, on passage to the Falklands. At 18 he was at the relief of Quebec in 1775. His actions during the subsequent operations on the American Lakes and at Saratoga, the battle in which his youngest brother John was killed, earned him promotion to Lieutenant.

When, at the start of the war with France in 1793, Edward was appointed to his first command of a frigate, the *Nymphe* (36 guns; 220 crew), experienced seamen were in short supply. He tried to solve his manning problem by enlisting to his ship's company some eighty Cornish miners together with his brother, Israel, as gunnery officer and a cousin, Lieutenant Richard Pellew. It was only a partial success as fifty of the miners took neither to the sea nor to naval discipline and jumped ship at the first port! With the rest of this untried but doughty crew he

---

[4] The inhabitants of Breage (and its neighbour Germoe) were infamous for the barbarity they showed to sailors when they plundered vessels wrecked on their shore. "God keep us from rocks and shelving sands, and save us from Breage and Germoe men's hands".

then put out from Falmouth and, soon after, in a bloody action in the Channel in which 23 of them were killed, they achieved the first British success of the war by capturing the *Cleopatra* (40 guns; 320 crew), considered the finest frigate of the French fleet. The whole nation saw it as a good omen and Edward and his crew were fêted among general rejoicing. At Plymouth three years later he was again in the news when almost single-handedly he rescued the passengers from the *Dutton*, a transport ship, which was being dashed to pieces in a winter storm under the walls of the Royal Citadel.

Such feats of courage and leadership were almost commonplace in Edward's long career. Naval historians call him "the finest sea officer of his age" and certainly his exploits at sea during the American and Napoleonic Wars made him a national hero and the most famous Cornishman of his time. Even the fictional hero "Horatio Hornblower", according to the author, learned his seamanship from "Pellew of the *Indefatigable*"! His competence and strength commanded great respect from his sailors but little affection. He never became the romantic idol that Nelson was, yet he was a better seaman and a less erratic servant of the Admiralty. He too was heaped with the honours of his own and many other countries that had been our allies in the 22 year long struggle against the French, and he became the first Viscount Exmouth. On his death not only the Pellew family but the whole of Cornwall mourned, and Philippa later named her new home on The Terrace at Chacewater after him - Exmouth House.

The earliest record of the Pellews at sea is of Captain William Pellew, Edward's great great grandfather, who had a house in Plymouth during the Civil War. William's overt loyalty to the King had "made him so obnoxious to the republicans of Plymouth that the mob assaulted him on the Hoe and plundered his house". The Pellews still have "a small piece of antique plate bearing the date 1645" which was the only article of value saved on that occasion. When Charles II commissioned the building of the Royal Citadel on Plymouth Hoe in 1665 he made sure that its guns, as well as pointing out to sea, would also overlook that disloyal city!

Both of Captain William Pellew's sons, Charles and George, went to sea in the second half of the 17th century. Charles, the elder, was a shipmaster out of Falmouth carrying tin to London whose only son aged seven was drowned on one of his father's voyages. George, the commander of a Privateer, had a son, Humphry Pellew, who became a merchant seaman and later a shipowner trading out of Falmouth to the American colonies. He purchased a 2000 acre tobacco plantation on Kent Island in Maryland, but the family later forfeited it to the colonists during the American War of Independence. It is said that part of the town of Annapolis Royal stands on what was once Pellew property.

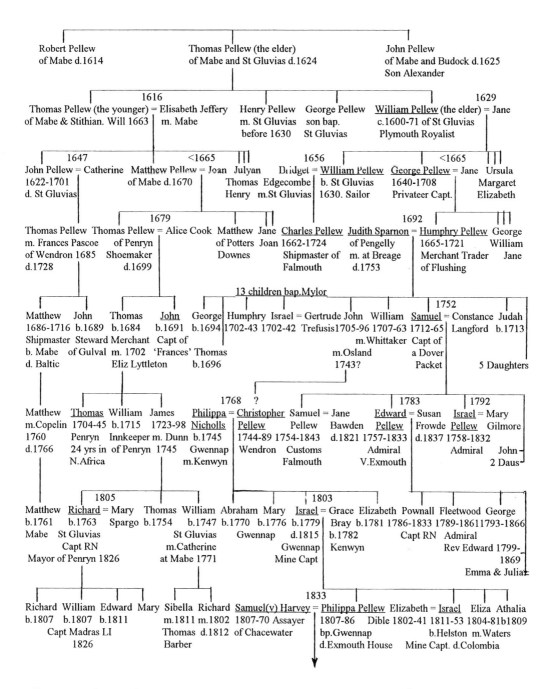

Sketch Pedigree of the Pellew descent down to Philippa Pellew 1807-86 of Chacewater

Characters who are referred to in the text of Chapter 6 are <u>underlined</u>

This chart is continued on page 36.

Back at home, Humphry together with Samuel Trefusis, his local MP and owner of the land, built the village of Flushing in a pleasant spot on the north side of the Penryn creek opposite Falmouth. It was to Flushing that many of the Falmouth Packet captains came to live as did Humphry himself with his wife, Judith Sparnon, and their large family of 13 children. Three of their nine sons were lost at sea. It is said that only their seventh son, Samuel the Captain of a Dover Packet, gave them grandchildren, among whom were Edward, the future Lord Exmouth, and his younger brother, Israel. Edward was also to make his home in Flushing - at No. 5/6 St Peter's Terrace.

Israel Pellew as a naval officer was rather overshadowed by the brilliant Edward. Whereas his two older brothers were described as 'sedate' (Samuel) and 'bold' (Edward), Israel, who had flaming red hair and a temper to match, was 'reckless' and 'profligate'. When brother Edward needed him to join the crew of the *Nymphe*, he was found tasting the pleasures of Ireland in a Cork bar! Edward's influence brought Israel promotion despite some major misfortunes in his career. In 1796 while docked at Plymouth prior to sailing, his ship the *Alphion* (32 guns) was completely destroyed in an accident with gunpowder causing the death of some 260 people. A friend with whom Israel had been dining in his cabin was killed while, extraordinarily, he himself recovered from his injuries having been blown out of a port onto the deck of an adjoining hulk. The crew of his next ship, the *Greyhound*, mutinied off Plymouth and "sent him on shore". Three years later in the *Cleopatra* (32 guns) he ran aground in the Bahamas, remaining fast for three days until he was forced to throw the guns and part of the ballast overboard. His moment finally came when at the battle of Trafalgar, as Captain of the *Conqueror* (74 guns), he captured the *Bucentaure* (80 guns), the flagship of Admiral Villeneuve who commanded the combined French and Spanish fleets.

The hazards of life at sea in the 18th century were not confined to war, shipwreck, mutiny and explosion. Piracy, an enterprise not unknown in Cornwall, was an ever present threat to merchant traders in some waters. In 1715 young Thomas Pellew of Penryn aged just 11 was captured by Moors on the Barbary coast off Cape Finisterre. He was accompanying his uncle John, the captain of the *Frances* out of Falmouth, taking a cargo of pilchards to Genoa. Thomas and his uncle found themselves in the filthy dungeons of Morocco where so many other Christian sailors had come to a miserable end. John Pellew succumbed there but Thomas, because of his youth, went as a slave to the son of the Sultan at Meknes near Fez, was induced to become a Muslim, learned Arabic and in due course became a soldier in the Sultan's army helping put down the frequent insurrections that were an integral part of Moorish government. After many adventures he finally succeeded in escaping. When he walked into his parents home at Penryn they failed to recognise him. He had been away for 24 years!

This picture of a frigate by "the Admiral" is thought to be of the *Squirrel* (20 guns), which in 1793 was Israel Pellew's first wartime command as Captain.
(Photo: Richard F Harvey)

Few sailors who fell into the hands of pirates along the Barbary coast survived to write a book about it, as did Thomas Pellew. However there is a certain justice in the way this awful trade in human misery was ended in 1816 by none other than a member of Thomas' family, Admiral Edward Pellew. It was the crowning success of Lord Exmouth's long career when, as an old seadog of nearly sixty, he had the task of persuading the Dey of Algiers to release 1600 British subjects imprisoned there. One cannot but admire the way he achieved it, first by negotiation and then with a judicious use of naval power against Algiers town from a confined area of sea. He had the fire of six British warships and a Dutch squadron. The effect on their town of such force at close quarters so impressed the Berbers that not only were the Dey's prisoners immediately released but slavery was abolished along the whole Barbary coast resulting in freedom for as many as 3000 Christian slaves.

The only Pellew heirloom to have come down to the Harveys is a little picture from the wall of Exmouth House which belonged to Philippa (see page 49). It is of a British square rigged man-of-war (small 6th rate) with the 'Blue Peter' on the foremast and 'Red Ensign' at the stern. According to Aunt Milly Harvey (1844-1944), it was painted by "the Admiral". It is thought to be by Edward's brother, Admiral Israel Pellew, and of the frigate *Squirrel* (20 guns) which in 1793 was his first wartime command as a captain.

This link to Israel Pellew is interesting. No baptismal record for Philippa's father, Israel, can be found and there is some evidence suggesting that he was the illegitimate son of his namesake Israel Pellew, the future Admiral, who at the relevant time in 1778 was a 20 year old midshipman on home leave after his ship the *Flora* had been scuttled off Rhode Island in the American war. Both putative father and son have the same two Christian names, 'Isaac Israel', names which are very rare among the Pellews and uncommon in Cornwall. Whether or not this theory of illegitimacy is true, we know that Israel, the son, was brought up by Christopher Pellew and his wife, Philippa Nicholls, whose children were about his age (see the Pellew sketch pedigree at page 47). In 1791 Israel was a witness at his widowed foster-mother's marriage to James Treviarian, a 91 year old bachelor from Kea, at which the bride was less than half her new and presumably rich husband's age!

A clue to the Pellew family's origins may lie in the name itself. Although it is now generally found as 'Pellew' or 'Pellow(e)', the variants of its spelling in earlier years are legion. In the baptismal records of Humphry Pellew's family of 13 children, the name is spelt in seven different ways. Edward Osler in 1835 wrote that the probable origin was the Norman name 'Pelleu' and to this day the family persist in pronouncing their name as 'Pell-oo' with the emphasis on the second syllable in the French way. Presuming the name to be Norman-French then various alternative derivations, none of them complimentary, are suggested by Reaney and others:-

A Bald man. A nickname from the French 'Pellé'.
A Stealthy person or **Slippery customer**. From a Norman variant of 'Pedley'.
Wolf skin. From the Old French 'Pel de lou'.

Chapter 7

QUAINT CUSTOMS, COOL CHARACTERS
Hichens & Penrose

It is difficult to disentangle the many different branches and blood lines of Cornish families of the 18th and 19th centuries. For generations many of them remained in much the same area and grew abundantly. When William Pellew Harvey married Elizabeth Hichens at Illogan in 1889 he was marrying into not one but two great Cornish dynasties.

Elizabeth's father was Richard Smith Hichens, an assayer, of Trengweath, Redruth, and her mother was Harriet, the daughter of John and Nancy Penrose of The Square, Redruth. In Elizabeth therefore were combined both Hichens and Penrose, huge family groups who could trace their origins back to prosperous 17th century figures, Richard Penrose a tinner of Redruth who died there in 1691 and John Hichens who was mayor of St Ives in 1664.

Richard Smith Hichens 1827-1907,
Assayer of Trengweath, Redruth
and husband of Harriet Penrose.

Elizabeth Hichens 1863-1954, his daughter,
and the wife of William Pellew-Harvey.
(Photos: Sir John Knill)

The name Hichens means "son of Richard" or "son of Hugh". The family with which we are concerned worked for many generations in the mines or on the waterfront of St Ives. It was Elizabeth's great grandfather, another John Hichens born there a hundred years after the mayor, who took his family to Redruth where his wife, Elizabeth Smith, had inherited property at Tregoy (Tregea?) in Illogan. John's departure from St Ives was followed by that of his first cousin, Robert Hichens, who at the age of 17 decided he would leave Cornwall to seek his fortune in London. Robert later wrote of seeing his grandmother, Mary Hichens, in St Ives before he left, *"I knelt at her feet to receive her blessing and had the happiness of hearing her say that I had never given her a moments pain but from ill health. I never saw her afterwards but her memory is still inexpressibly dear to me"*. In those days fortunate indeed was a young man like Robert who could depend on the cohesion and strength, particularly financial strength, of the wider family when he was starting out in the world.

Within six years Robert had established a successful stockbroking firm, Hichens & Harrison. In 1841 it was he who uncovered one of the most spectacular frauds of the 19th century involving forged Exchequer Bills amounting to many millions of pounds in today's values. The chief perpetrator, one J. Beaumont Smith, was sentenced to transportation for life! This did the Hichens name no harm and the business continued to flourish to the great benefit of Robert's branch of the family. Three of his four sons went into the church but he was joined in the City for five years by his younger brother, William, and then by his nephews, Jack and Andrew Hichens, who in due course became respectively chairman and trustee of the Stock Exchange.

Robert left a journal in which he described his memories of earlier generations of the Hichens family, their customs and the tribulations they had to face in 18th century St Ives. The quotations printed in this chapter in italics are from his stories with their mixture of family devotion and a rather businesslike approach to marriage and remarriage. There was for example the sad occasion of the burial in 1736 of his great grandfather's only daughter, Polly. She was unmarried, just 20, when she caught a chill dutifully looking after her parents when they were both sick. *"In those days the family were always buried at night by torchlight, and the body was born to the church not by hired bearers but by intimate friends of the deceased who after the funeral returned to the house where a cold collation was prepared. When the bearers were returned and seated the father came into the room and standing at the top of the table said 'I bid you welcome to Polly's wedding supper', whereupon he burst into a flood of* tears and rushed out of the room. *He was never seen to smile afterwards*". The poor man's grief was compounded three years later when his two sons of a similar age were in France learning the language. They went out shooting together and an accident occurred in which one killed the other.

Their elder brother Richard was a surgeon who married late in life. His son, Robert, was born only the year before his father died and was adopted by his mother's sister who was the wife of Sir John Dick, Consul in Leghorn. Robert *"became a Captain in the Navy at a very early age but Sir John Dick finding him incurably addicted to drunkenness, the vice of the age, cast him off after paying large debts for him twice. Robert retired to Aberdeen upon his half pay where he died. He was a very brave man, a perfect gentleman in manner and a good officer, but drunkenness ruined all. He was my godfather and I was called Robert after him, being carried to the font dressed in the same baby clothes as he had worn at his christening*".

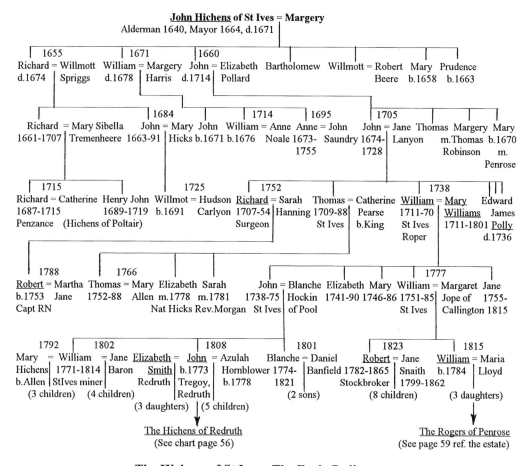

The Hichens of St Ives - The Early Pedigree
Connects with the chart of the Redruth Branch later in this chapter (page 56)
Characters who are referred to in the text are underlined

53

Robert remembers his grandfather, William Hichens (1711-70), who was *"bred to be a roper"* in St Ives. *"I am told he was a man of great sweetness of temper, with a rich vein of humour and universally beloved. His kindness to the poor was almost beyond his means and I am thankful to say that when he was carried to the grave, many of the poor followed weeping, saying 'there goes the poor man's friend'. The same tribute was borne to my father, and God grant it may be said of me and my descendants!"*

Robert tells of the misfortunes of his grandmother's father, John Williams, *"a considerable ship owner and for many years a man of very good property at St Ives"*. He had three sons, all the captains of St Ives ships. The eldest was drowned when his ship was wrecked off the coast of Holland. War then broke out (probably the War of Austrian Succession in 1742) and, as a result, all his ships except two were wrecked or taken by the enemy (France again). Thereupon he sent his sons to the Mediterranean with his two remaining ships loaded with pilchards. As he said, except for his daughter, *"all he had was in that venture, two sons, two ships, two cargoes"*. They never returned and the disaster *"broke the firm-hearted old man down"* in health, strength and fortune. His son-in-law's response to these events was to invite him to share their home. But his wife said *"'Father is a very morose man and you will never be able to put up with his temper'. 'Yes I shall my dear. He is your father and that is enough, and though we have but slender means God will make it up to our children'."*

Many years later the fate of these two ships was discovered when *"my grandfather's brother was taken captive by Algerine pirates, carried into the interior and confined in a dungeon lined with lead. Amongst many sad memorials 'graved in the metal were"* the names of John William's two missing sons.

Two descendants and namesakes of Robert Hichens, the writer of the journal, became well known in the 20th century. One, his great grandson, lost his life at sea during the Second World War. Lt Cdr Robert Hichens, DSO DSC (1909-43), the most decorated officer of the RNVR, became famous for his motor gunboat operations in the Channel and against the enemy coasts of France, Belgium and Holland, often by night. Most of the tactics used by these small ships that proved so successful were developed and practised by him and he rose to command a flotilla of them before he was killed in action in 1943. The other, Robert Smythe Hichens (1864-1950) was a popular novelist and amateur musician whose best known book was *The Garden of Allah*.

New research has shown that a 'Robert Hichens', origin unknown, was the Quartermaster on the Titanic in 1912 and was steering the ship (under orders from the Officer of the Watch) when she struck the iceberg!

Descendants of John Hichens, born St Ives 1773

His father had just been killed in a fall from his horse when John Hichens of St Ives took his young family to settle at Tregoy near Redruth in the 1790s. Happily their arrival there coincided with the expansion of mining in which they were to benefit for two further generations. The photograph below, taken in the 1870s, is of two of John's sons and two grandsons, one a doctor, the other, Richard Smith Hichens, an assayer, with his wife Harriet Penrose.

The Hichens of Redruth c.1870. Seated with Harriet is her father-in-law John Hichens b.1796 with his two sons Dr James (left) and Richard Smith Hichens flanking his half brother Richard. See chart on page 56.   (Photo: Sir John Knill)

Richard's mother, Elizabeth Stacey, had a nephew the same age as Richard who used to visit them when he was on long leaves from India. This was Stephen Townsend, a doctor in the Indian Medical Service who, at about the time this photograph was taken, was fighting in the Second Afghan War in which he was severely wounded. He was described as "a tall substantial man given to wearing full uniform and on operations used to trot alongside General 'Bob' Roberts, the hero of Kabul and Kandahar. The General said that he had him ride beside him not especially for his company but to draw the enemy's fire!" Stephen became a Surgeon-General in 1880. His grandson was Group Captain Peter Townsend DSO DFC who became an Equerry to the King and was later engaged to Princess Margaret until it was decided that his divorced state disqualified him from marriage to the Queen's sister.

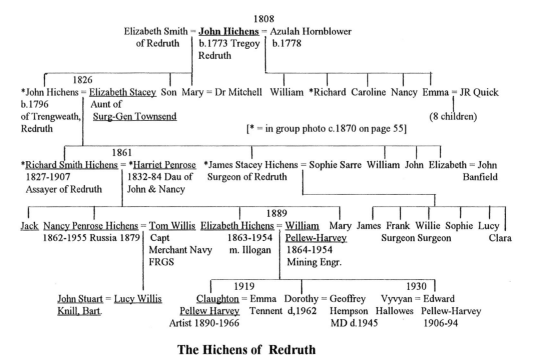

The Hichens of Redruth
This chart continues the earlier one on page 53 and links into that on page 58
Characters who are referred to in the text are <u>underlined</u>

Richard Smith Hichens and Harriet Penrose had two surviving daughters and a son Jack. Nothing is known of Jack except that he was "a bad lot". The younger daughter, Elizabeth Hichens, as we have seen went to Canada with her husband William Pellew Harvey in 1890. Her elder sister, Nancy Penrose Hichens, a strong adventurous lady, had flown the nest a decade before when at 17 she went off alone to Russia as a governess. Rumour has it that she was once engaged to her cousin Robert Smythe Hichens, the novelist; but in Russia she met and married the gallant captain of a British merchant ship. With Tom Willis she sailed the seas for several years, later accompanied by their young daughter

Lucy. Tom, who first learned his trade back in the days of sail, was a master mariner and a fine and courageous sailor. He was the recipient of the Royal Humane Society medal for saving life at sea and was made a Fellow of the Royal Geographic Society. He was known among the females of the family as a "bottom pincher", a trait that as far as we know has not been handed down!

Lucy married into the inventive but eccentric Knill family who are of old Welsh stock. Her father-in-law, Sir John Knill, had been Lord Mayor of London. In St Ives today they still remember a John Knill of the 18th century who was their collector of customs for twenty years and mayor of the town in 1767. In his memory on nearby Worvas Hill stands the John Knill monument, a large steeple-shaped granite mausoleum. He endowed the celebrations that have been held faithfully at St Ives every five years since 1801, even during wartime. The ceremony is a strange one involving ten girls dressed in white, escorted by the mayor, vicar, customs officer and two elderly widows led by a fiddler. They parade round the town and then after the girls dance at "Knill's Steeple" the whole company sing the Hundredth Psalm. Is it not a curious thing that a wealthy customs officer should be so honoured in a land with such a strong fair-trade (smuggling) tradition?

In his journal Robert Hichens, the London stockbroker, wrote of this John Knill, who was his mother's half-brother, that he was also *at one period Inspector General of the Customs in the British West India Islands, and subsequently private secretary to the Earl of Buckinghamshire when Lord Lieutenant of Ireland*. Clearly a man of some influence, John Knill died unmarried in 1811. He left his considerable property to his half-brother whose only daughter Mary, Robert's first cousin, married the heir to the Penrose estate, one of the finest in west Cornwall (described on page 59).

Penrose of Redruth
The Family of Harriet Penrose 1832-84

Penrose was the family of Elizabeth Hichens' mother, Harriet who figures in the group photograph earlier in this chapter. The Penrose name is a local one meaning "top end of the heath" and was very widespread in west Cornwall. Harriet Penrose's branch of the family were settled in and around Redruth from at least the 17th century, and mostly described themselves as 'tinners' or later 'assayers'. They were not without means; a Will of 1742 (that of Harriet's great great grandmother, Jane Penrose) shows the family then had shares in at least six different mining concerns. We know also that Harriet's brother, John Farran Penrose born 1829, an assayer, cashier, magistrate and owner of a Redruth mining company (John F Penrose & Sons), lived in style "in a large house with servants and a private chapel in the grounds".

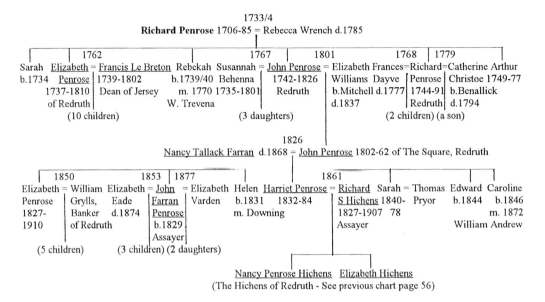

1733/4
Richard Penrose 1706-85 = Rebecca Wrench d.1785

1762		1767	1801	1768	1779	
Sarah b.1734 1737-1810 of Redruth	Elizabeth Penrose = Francis Le Breton 1739-1802 Dean of Jersey (10 children)	Rebekah 1735-1801	Susannah b.1739/40 Behenna m.1770 W. Trevena (3 daughters)	John Penrose 1742-1826 Redruth = Elizabeth Frances Williams Dayve b.Mitchell d.1777 d.1837	Richard Penrose 1744-91 Redruth = Catherine Christoe 1749-77 b.Benallick d.1794 (2 children)	Arthur (a son)

1826
Nancy Tallack Farran d.1868 = John Penrose 1802-62 of The Square, Redruth

1850	1853	1877			1861			
Elizabeth Penrose 1827-1910 = William Grylls, Banker of Redruth (5 children)	Elizabeth Eade d.1874 = John Farran Penrose b.1829 Assayer (3 children)	= Elizabeth Varden (2 daughters)	Helen b.1831 m. Downing	Harriet Penrose 1832-84 = Richard S Hichens 1840-78 Assayer	Richard 1827-1907 Assayer	Sarah = Thomas Pryor	Edward b.1844	Caroline b.1846 m. 1872 William Andrew

Nancy Penrose Hichens   Elizabeth Hichens
(The Hichens of Redruth - See previous chart page 56)

Penrose of Redruth - Harriet Penrose's Family
Characters who are referred to in the text are underlined

Elizabeth Hichens was a painter in water-colours and it is said that her talent for art and that of her elder son Claughton Pellew came from the Penrose side. Her husband William, always immaculately dressed, was professional, precise and very punctual, while Elizabeth was the opposite, easy-going, amusing, artistic, liberal and generally late. She took especial pleasure in her home and yet, such was her restless spirit, insisted on moving every few years, invariably refurnishing each new place from scratch with no expense spared. Many was the time that William, arriving back from a long absence abroad, had difficulty finding where he was living!

Lillie Langtry
(Photo: Daily Telegraph).

It is thanks to Elizabeth Hichens' great grandfather John Penrose (1742-1826), in whose Bible is a family record, that we know much of the Redruth branch of the Penroses. The details are sparse but from further research we were able to confirm an unlikely but persistent story linking the family to 'Jersey Lillie'. It was found that this John Penrose had an elder sister Elizabeth who had fallen for a young curate, Francis Le Breton, just over from Jersey. They married and had a family of ten children. One of her great granddaughters was the beautiful Lillie Langtry (born Emily Charlotte Le Breton[5] 1853-1929), celebrated actress and mistress of the Prince of Wales, later King Edward VII.

We failed to substantiate a story of another Penrose link, this time with "Q", the pseudonym for the famous Cornish writer Arthur Quiller-Couch (1863-1944), but instead discovered an ancestor of his, James Couch, who was Captain Israel Pellew's First Lieutenant in the *Conqueror* at Trafalgar.

The Penrose estate, referred to earlier, is a particularly handsome property (of more than 10,000 acres in 1880) which overlooks Loe Pool, a large freshwater lake near Porthleven. The estate was once owned by the Sithney branch of the Penrose family, but in 1770 after the male line had died out it was acquired by one Hugh Rogers whose descendants still live there today (although the family gave much of the land to the National Trust in 1974). Such continuity is exceptional in the Cornwall of this period which saw the upheaval of a society that had endured for centuries past. There now remain surprisingly few of the once prolific Penrose family in Cornwall. They, like the Hichens, the Pellews, the Harveys of Chacewater, and many of the old Cornish names, have been carried to other parts of the world. It would be a pity if some echo of their Cornish inheritance were not to reach them there.

---

[5] 'Lillie' Langtry 1853-1929 was the only daughter of William Le Breton, Dean of Jersey, and had six brothers. She was a serious actress with a career spanning 36 years and the author of two autobiographical books. She had a daughter in 1881 who was said to be the son of Prince Louis of Battenburg, the nephew of the Prince of Wales. After the death of her reclusive husband Edward Langtry in 1897 she married a Baronet 19 years her junior.

PART 3

SUPPLEMENT

-o-o-o-o-o-o-o-

MODERN SKETCHES

The Return 1925,
a wood engraving by Claughton Pellew based on Mousehole.

A SHY CORNISHMAN

The artist Claughton Pellew 1890-1966

Cornwall has been the inspiration for generations of artists and writers. Here is an exception, a Cornishman, one of the last of the Harveys to be born in Cornwall, who by circumstance became exposed to quite different artistic influences and, instead of returning to his native land, chose to live in isolation on the windy north Norfolk coast. From there his visions of the countryside around him began to flow like a dream.

"He seemed fated to work for and help others and denied himself the full exercise of his talents. Poor dear man he was the most unselfish of beings", wrote the artist John Nash of his lifelong friend Claughton Pellew. Claughton was a landscape artist who sought obscurity but found himself playing an important role when his perceptions of English pastoral peace and harmony, translated into water-colour and wood engraving, led the way out of the trauma inflicted on the country by the First World War. Even today, sixty years after the main body of his work was completed, his burning affection for the rural scenes of the past shines through.

The brothers Paul and John Nash, who became two of the most influential English landscape painters of this century, were each of them fired up by the young Claughton's romantic approach and by the intensity of his love for the countryside and its features. Paul trained with Claughton at the Slade in London, where their contemporaries included such future luminaries of the art world as Ben Nicholson, Stanley Spencer and Christopher Nevinson.

In 1912 Paul spent a walking holiday with Claughton staying at the latter's lodgings in Norfolk, and in his autobiography wrote of him: *"He was the first creature of a truly poetic cast of mind that I had met. We had much in sympathy, although I had more to learn than I could possibly give. His own work was remarkable for a searching intensity both in thought and technique. It was full of suggestion to my unformed mind"*...."*I was shaken within; a new vibration had been set up"*. Paul's younger brother, John Nash, acknowledged that he too owed Claughton *"a great debt for his encouragement and advice at an impressionable age and his more mature views opened out a new world for me while his accomplished technique in his water-colours and engravings set me a standard to be achieved"*.

Claughton Pellew, *Self-portrait* 1912,
red chalk on paper (Anne Tennent).

How was it then that an artist, clearly one of distinction and influence, who received such accolades from his peers has remained comparatively unknown? The answer seems to be that he was, in both a spiritual and artistic sense, a casualty of the First World War which caused him to withdraw into a form of self-imposed obscurity. Not until Anne Stevens at the Ashmolean in Oxford mounted an exhibition of his wood engravings in 1987, followed three years later by full exhibitions of his work held in London, Norfolk, Sussex and Devon, have Claughton's remarkable talents come to be more widely admired. And now an exhibition of his work is to be mounted for the first time in his native Cornwall in 1999 by the Royal Cornwall Museum at Truro, and will then move on to other West Country venues.

Born at Redruth in 1890, the great grandson of Samuel(v) Harvey and Philippa Pellew of Chacewater, Claughton was the last of this old Cornish family to be born in the Duchy. He and his parents, the peripatetic mining engineer William Pellew-Harvey and the amusing, artistic Elizabeth Hichens, became part of the great Cornish exodus. It was thus that Claughton spent his early years in the mountains of British Columbia. The isolation and beauty of that environment made a great impression on him and he developed there a fiercely independent attitude to life which in later years lay uneasily alongside the gentle nature of this essentially shy and sensitive man.

The family returned home in 1901 not to Cornwall but to London where Claughton's father set up a thriving mining consultancy. Much to William Pellew-Harvey's disappointment the young Claughton was far too unworldly to be tempted into the family business; he dropped the Harvey from his surname and left home to study art. Four years at the Slade was followed by the transcendent experience of seeing the art of the Florentine Quattrocento and visits to Assisi where the town's historical and religious associations overwhelmed him. On his return he wholeheartedly embraced religious symbolism in his work and converted to Catholicism. The year was 1914.

When war came Claughton, a pacifist like many of his artist contemporaries, became a conscientious objector and refused to be drafted. For this he suffered grievously in labour camps and prisons in the south of England, Scotland, Yorkshire and finally in Dartmoor. These were miserable, lonely and traumatic years. On release his alienation from society, deepened by knowing that better-connected Bloomsbury Group pacifists like Mark Gertler and Duncan Grant had avoided imprisonment, was almost complete. John Nash described it as *"a sense of permanent isolation from which Claughton never recovered"*.

In 1919 he married another artist, Emma ('Kechie') Tennent and they settled in a remote corner of north Norfolk where, apart from family visits to his native Cornwall and holidays in the Bavarian Alps where he could recreate his British Columbian boyhood, they remained for the rest of their lives. They lived the simple life using bicycles for transport and, until 1955, oil lamps for light and with their privacy protected by a flock of geese. Norfolk may seem an odd choice for an expatriate Cornish artist but it was in part the trees that attracted him. *"The trees slanting one way, their branches welded together in tortuous forms by the relentless winds"* became a characteristic of his landscapes.

The Train 1920, a watercolour with ink and gouache (Hove Museum & Art Gallery)

It was in the 1920s that Claughton began the most productive part of his working life. It was a time when the world of nature and especially the English countryside and its landscapes became the panacea for the ills that war had inflicted. This movement represented a step back, reverence for the past and its traditions and an escape from war and the modern industrial machine. The burning affection that Claughton expressed in his English rural landscapes, the romantic intensity of his art and his skill at the traditional craft of wood engraving, all equipped him to be at the centre of this movement.

One of his best known village designs is *The Return 1925* (page 62) which is based on the little Cornish fishing port of Mousehole. The houses are grouped to show the closeness of the community, and the chimney smoke rising vertically emphasises the peacefulness of the scene. The whole feeling is of order and tradition with people, in this case fishermen, working with nature. Among his water-colours *The Train 1920* (page 65), is familiar, one of a few to feature an infernal machine. Here he depicts the night train which he could see from his home, not as an alien element but in peaceful harmony with the shepherd and his flock; all is calm despite the evidence of wind in the "*tortuous form*" of the trees.

By the depression of the 1930s Claughton's productive years were over. Interest in country themes had waned as had the demand for prints, but he was loathe to leave his rural idyll to gain the stimulation to strike out in a new direction. Then war returned again and poor Pellew, who was known to have German friends and to speak the language, was arrested as a suspected spy and held until his blameless British status could be established.

Despite his sad life, lived for the most part in self-imposed obscurity, this kind, unassuming and gifted man has left us some wonderful pictures that epitomise that period between the wars when his images of rural peace helped eclipse the memories of bloody conflict. His search for solace in a savage world led to some saintly visions of a land now forgotten but well worth remembering.

THE FAMILY MAN

Edward Pellew-Harvey 1906-94

"Ted" Pellew-Harvey, the younger brother of Claughton by 16 years, was the last true Cornishman to be born into the family. His parents were then living in the soft leafy London suburb of Blackheath where the rigours of the Canadian Rockies and the hardships of Cornish mining in decline were a distant memory. Ted was spoilt unmercifully by his older sisters who doted on him. Only occasionally did the world outside break into the younger children's comfortable lives; when for instance their father William returned from one of his long mining trips and spoke of the distant places and outlandish people that he had seen. Ted was alone in his attic nursery at Blackheath when he saw the first Zeppelin air raid on London at the start of the Great War 1914-18, a sight he never forgot.

He was sent off to boarding school at Uppingham from which in due course he emerged unencumbered by qualifications but with the capacity to enjoy a hectic social life and with no desire to follow his father into the family business. Ted was a handsome man who like his father took pride in his appearance, was well organised and punctual to a fault. He had a most attractive and engaging personality and, despite the loss of most of his hair in his twenties, the ladies always loved him. A charming and friendly man he adored social gatherings, especially informal family occasions or lunchtime at the pub. The best of companions he was amusing and sympathetic and quickly able to transcend any age gap. He had a disarming sense of humour, an infectious giggle like his elder brother, and was given to childish practical jokes which made him a favourite with the young. His grandchildren remember with fondness the early morning shopping expeditions shared with him, during which a long visit to the sweet shop was always in the programme.

At the age of twenty Ted was driving a London bus during the General Strike. He eventually found work in the gas industry and at the time of his wedding in 1930 he was a manager with the Mitcham Gas Company. He used to say of his marriage to Vyvyan Hallowes, the younger daughter of a Devon clergyman, that it was the best day's work he ever did. Two years later, aged 26, he was made general manager of the Wandsworth & District Gas Company, the youngest general manager in the industry. He would be amused to read of the huge salaries that are now paid to our gas chiefs!

Ted and Vyvyan Pellew-Harvey on their Golden Wedding Day at Braceby in 1980 (Photo: Barbara Pellew-Harvey).

Like his father he enjoyed change and travel and it was not long before he left London to work for Norfolk Canneries (partly owned by his father), settling at North Walsham, not far from his brother Claughton. When war came again Ted, who was in a reserved occupation, served as a sergeant in the Home Guard. He was an inveterate storyteller and many of the experiences portrayed in TV's "Dad's Army" seem also to have happened to him! Indeed he wrote short stories some of which were published in Blackwood's Magazine for which he used the pen name "Edward Le Breton" after his mother's distant relative, the famous Lillie Langtry née Le Breton. He and Vyvyan were then bringing up four young children in wartime Norfolk.

The local fruit farm that Ted purchased after the war failed to flourish and in 1952 he moved his growing family out to Kenya where he started working in a new pineapple operation at Kilifi for Kenya Canners, later moving to be managing director of East African Diatomite Industries. He always said that his Kenya years were the happiest of his life. He adored Africa and had extraordinary ability to get the very best from his staff irrespective of their race or creed. The country was just recovering from the Mau Mau troubles and so the family had to learn to defend itself with occasional shooting practices, a dangerous activity at the best of times. Vyvyan invariably shut her eyes and looked the opposite way when she was about to fire her pistol, and Ted kept his locked in the whisky cabinet so he could check it each day! It was fortunate that neither of them were ever attacked.

After independence the activities of the African trade unions affected Ted's business and in 1967 the family, now with the addition of Stephen who was born in Kenya, returned to England. Ted and Vyvyan eventually retired to the little village of Braceby in Lincolnshire where they spent 17 happy years. Finally they moved south again to Dorchester-on-Thames where in 1990 they celebrated their Diamond Wedding among their 5 children, 19 grandchildren and 2 great grandchildren (by 1997 this last figure has risen to 11) joined by Vyvyan's brother, Michael Hallowes, and his son Paul. This total may fall short of the 63 grandchildren of Ted's Cornish ancestor Samuel(iv) Harvey of Chacewater but it still looks like a very sturdy foundation for the future.

Ted's life was devoted to the love and care of his family and of Vyvyan, who supported him so loyally through the difficult times, especially during the increasing blindness of his last few years, and shared with him the many blessings that came their way in 64 years of happy married life. Among those blessings Ted would certainly count moments contemplating a favourite view. Two in particular are recalled: one in Kenya was the view from his house overlooking the Rift Valley, and the other from his son's home in France over Lake Geneva and the mountains on the far shore. A sunset salute with a glass in his hand!

A MUSICAL LADY

Rosemary Olivia Harvey, born Newport 1918

Music has been the theme of Rosemary Harvey's life. It could hardly have been otherwise. A Welsh mother and a Cornish father, who sang, played the piano, loved opera and became a musical journalist, occasionally broadcasting on classical music for the BBC[6], gave her a good Celtic start. Her artistic interest was fostered by their encouragement and by having a London home with access to all of the city's exciting musical and theatrical life when she was growing up between the wars. Operas, ballets, concerts, theatres and galleries became an integral part of her life.

The musical origins of Rosemary's branch of the Harvey family go further back (See pedigree chart on page 35). Her father, Hugh Harvey and his two older brothers, Fred and Ernest, had been brought up by her grandparents in London near their aunt Nanny Harvey, the daughter of Samuel(iv) of Chacewater. It was probably Nanny who first brought music into the family by marrying Théophile Antoine, a Belgian professor of music who is thought to have been of Huguenot descent. The Antoines and their four melodious children had a strong influence on their young nephew, James ("Jimmy") Harvey, Rosemary's grandfather. He had come up from Chacewater to work as a clerk at the London end of the Great Western Railway which had recently extended its lines into Cornwall. In 1868 Jimmy and his bride Helen James of Truro came to live near the Antoines in Pimlico and thus was the love of music and especially of opera engendered in Rosemary's father and his two brothers. It never left them.

Rosemary's uncle Fred was a francophile bachelor. Along with this keen interest in music and the arts he was also a brilliant teacher especially of maths and science which he taught at a Southwark school. In 1912 he started his own school in Paris providing "individual tuition" for boys and girls of all ages working for English, French or American qualifications at any level from common entrance or matriculation to college, university or vocational entry. Architecture, archaeology, music and the arts were among many subjects that he offered, and his school flourished for nearly thirty years, finally closing in 1939. Fred was briefly interned by the Germans when they marched into Paris in 1941 but then released because of his age, 70. He vanished into the French countryside and nothing was heard of him until he appeared again three years

---

[6] Hugh Harvey was a contributor for many years to the BBC's "Collectors' Corner" classical record programme.

later when France was liberated. He had been befriended by a French family whose son he had coached. When he made one last visit to London after the war was over, it was not on his own account but to promote a young pianist, Raffi Petrossian, who had been his pupil - a fitting epitaph for this grand old teacher.

The Harveys of London 1913. At the back are the three brothers, from left Ernest, Fred and Hugh with Ernest's wife, Emmy and their baby Jack sitting in the centre flanked by the brothers' parents, James and Helen Harvey of Pimlico.   (Photo: Rosemary Morgan)

Fred and his two brothers were excellent linguists, especially Hugh who was a polyglot, fluent in French, Spanish (both the Castilian and South American dialects) and with good German and Italian; this gift was not inherited by his daughter Rosemary although she has been complimented on her pronunciation when she sings in Italian. Ernest, who was not a good correspondent, lost touch with his brothers having left London to live in Argentina and later New York where his third child was born in 1921. This left Rosemary the only Harvey of her generation in London. She was a keen dancer and inherited a beautiful soprano voice which was trained in the 'belcanto' style and has been a joy throughout her life. Any hopes she had of singing professionally were dashed by the outbreak of war when she was just 21 and by the death of her music teacher in 1940. Rosemary, who was working in a City bank when the war reached London, witnessed the nightly raids and devastation of the Blitz at its height. By 1942 she had joined the WAAF and was working in RAF operation rooms plotting the movement of our own and enemy aircraft, firstly in Anglesey helping the Navy to defend the Atlantic approaches and then back in London as part of the international planning team for the Normandy landings and after.

At the end of the war Rosemary married David Morgan, a Fleet Air Arm pilot who later became a test pilot for Vickers. It is no surprise to learn that each of their three children has an ear for music (one is a singer and another was a professional dancer) and Rosemary's fourteen year old granddaughter, Judy, plays the clarinet, saxophone and classical guitar![7]

Rosemary Olivia Harvey in WAAF uniform during the war   (Photo: Rosemary Morgan)

---

[7] In the interests of musical balance it should also be said that Rosemary's other grandchild, Adrian, plays "blues" guitar.

THE SUBMARINER
Richard Frederick Harvey, born Croydon 1926

Richard Frederick Harvey's father, 'Dick' was a graduate of the Royal College of Science, trained also as a surveyor and assayer of copper and silver and became a mining engineer. Over the next three decades this took him to almost every corner of the world where there were mines to be worked (See chapter 5, pages 41-43). Like the father, his son, Richard, also became an itinerant engineer, but of a very different sort

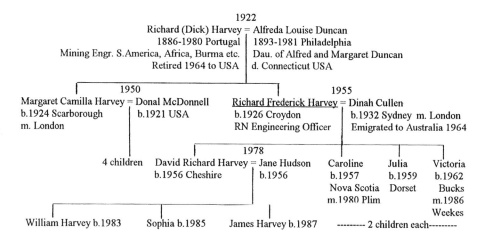

Descendants of Dick Harvey & Alfreda Duncan
Connects with the Harvey/Seymour chart on page 40

Within a few months of war breaking out in Europe in the autumn of 1939 Richard, aged 13 and his 15 year old sister Margaret Camilla Harvey ('Camilla' after her Portuguese grandmother) found themselves marooned with their parents near Oporto where their father had been working. The Spanish frontier was closed, German U-boats were sinking shipping in the Bay of Biscay and the invasion of France was imminent. It was not until February 1940 that the family, taking only what they could carry, were finally able to make the long hazardous journey home through Spain and France. They escaped just in time: by June 337,000 British and Allied troops had been evacuated from Dunkirk and France had capitulated.

At first they made their home in London with Richard and Margaret attending boarding schools on the south coast at Eastbourne. The schools were soon forced to close after the children had spent three successive nights in air raid shelters, and then with bombs falling on London each night the whole family moved out to Worcestershire where Dick had found work. Meanwhile Richard, despite his fractured education, had gained a scholarship to Downside, the Catholic school in Somerset, and from there he emerged in March 1944 aged 17, just a couple of months before D Day and with the end of the war in Europe more than a year away.

What more natural than at such a time this descendant of a long line of Cornish mining engineers should train as an engineer - in the Navy. Richard passed into the Royal Naval College, which was then not at Dartmouth but near Chester, and from there went to the RN Engineering College at Manadon in Devon where he graduated in 1945 soon after the Japanese surrender. It was therefore into a ravaged but more peaceful world that he set sail in the Aircraft Carrier *HMS Indomitable* on passage to the Far East to join his first ship the Battleship *Anson* in Sydney harbour as a Midshipman (E). Sydney must have impressed him for 18 years later he made it his home.

This first appointment took Richard and *HMS Anson* into Japanese waters where for some weeks they supported the army of occupation in the Inland Sea (between Shikoku and the main island of Honshu). He twice visited Hiroshima on which the first atomic bomb had been dropped nine months before, and, in the prosaic way of engineers, reported this city of 320,000 people "absolutely flat"[8]. He also saw Osaka, Kyoto and Tokyo before the ship took the long passage home to Portsmouth at the end of her commission.

After leaving *Anson* at Portsmouth in August 1946 Richard returned to the RN Engineering College at Plymouth for 15 months during which he was promoted to Sub Lieutenant. His next ship was the Cruiser *Phoebe* which he joined at Valetta and in which he gained his watchkeeping certificate. In May 1948 *Phoebe* was in the eastern Mediterranean helping to oversee the birth of the new state of Israel. Among her duties was the interception of ships carrying Jewish illegal emigrants to Palestine. Two years later Richard went as an instructor to the Apprentices Training School at Rosyth where he says he was put in charge of the brass band!

On leaving Rosyth in August 1951 he embarked on what was to be the final phase of his naval career. After three months specialist training at Portsmouth he was appointed Engineer Officer in the submarine *HMS Telemachus* based at Sydney. The six week voyage to join his new ship was to prove momentous in that on board *RMS Strathaird* he met his future wife, Dinah Cullen - just as his

---

[8] Hiroshima. The bare statistics of this awful event are that nearly 30% of the inhabitants were killed by the immediate effects of the bomb and four square miles of the city centre were completely destroyed with damage extending out for three miles.

parents had met crossing the Atlantic on the *Mauritania* thirty years before! Richard cannot have seen much of Dinah, a fifth generation Australian who lived in Sydney, for he spent 14 months away in Singapore, where *Telemachus* underwent a long refit, and on exercises off Hong Kong and with the US Fleet at Sasebo, Japan.

In December 1953 on the completion of his time in the Far East Richard took leave to return to UK via Fiji, Honolulu and the States where he stayed for three months with his sister and her American husband in Connecticut. A year later he was in the submarine *Turpin* on Arctic patrol off Murmansk to test Russian naval proficiency. There they remained for six weeks without surfacing and on one occasion were forced by "the enemy" to stay deep for an uncomfortable 72 hours. Richard had just found time the month before this patrol to marry Dinah in London and snatch a two day honeymoon in the Cotswolds!

The Battleship *HMS Anson* on the way home from Japan 1946 (Photo: Richard F Harvey)

There followed a shore appointment supervising submarine construction and refits at the Cammell Laird shipyard at Birkenhead after which Richard spent two years as Engineer Officer for the Submarine Squadron in Halifax, Nova Scotia where Dinah was able to join him. For his final two years in the Navy he was firstly in the submarine Depot Ship *Chaser* based at Portland, Dorset, and then with the Malta Squadron in *HMS Narvik*. He was just 35 with 17 years service when he retired in September 1961 having taken voluntary redundancy.

Richard then became a test engineer working for Carrier Engineering Ltd on their installations at the British Motor Corporation factory at Cowley in Oxford, and bought a home in Buckinghamshire. It was there at Christmas 1963 that he broke the news to the family that he and Dinah had decided to emigrate to Australia in the new year. It was a shock to his elderly parents but despite their age, Dick was then 77, they resolved that they too would emigrate to spend their last years near their daughter in Connecticut. And so it happened; the parents had 17 happy years together near Margaret in America, while Richard and Dinah, then with four children aged 8, 7, 5 and 2, left London by air for a new life in Sydney. They still live there in a suburb of the city called Double Bay which sounds a suitable spot for a sailor.

The T Class Submarine *HMS Turpin* in which Richard Harvey was on Arctic patrol off Murmansk in 1955 (Photo: Richard F Harvey)

THE TRADER

William ("Bill") Bernard Pellew-Harvey, born Norfolk 1941

In Bill Pellew-Harvey there is much of the restless spirit of his grandfather William after whom he was named (Pages 36-37 'William the Wanderer'). He was born in wartime Norfolk to Ted and Vyvyan in the same week that the Japanese attacked Pearl Harbour and brought America into the war - a portent perhaps of his subsequent capacity for finding his way into perilous situations.

1889
William Pellew-Harvey = Elizabeth Hichens
1864-1954. Mining Engineer.
In British Columbia 1889-1901
Mining Consultancy in the City of London until 1942
1863-1954, Dau. of Richard Smith Hichens,
Assayer of Portreath, & Harriet Penrose of Redruth
m. Illogan. Both d. at Hove Jan 1954
1919
Claughton Pellew = Emma Tennent
1890-1966 b.Redruth 1888-1968
Artist. d.Norfolk
Norah d.young
Helen d.1942
Dorothy = Geoffrey
b.Canada Hempson
d.1962 Hove MD d.1945
1930
Edward Pellew-Harvey = Grace Vyvyan
1906-94 b.Blackheath Hallowes b.1908
Norfolk, Kenya, Lincs Derbyshire
3rd 2nd 1st
Robin Addie = // Michael Ellison ≠ Elizabeth (Buffy) = Adrian Jepson
of Glasgow Solicitor of Wappenham Drowned 1939-45
Gillian = John Ellison
Living Norfolk Accountant
Son: William
Gillian Jepson ≠ Holgersson
Living Sweden Olympic
Daughter: Susie Horseman
Ann b.1932 6 children Berkshire
Judy b.1934 4 children Toronto
1966 1977
Maria Chedotal ≠ William Pellew-Harvey = Barbara McGrath
b.1941 Norfolk b.1953 Texas
International Business
Living California
Catherine b.1943 2 Daus. Portugal
1981
Stephen P-H = Anne Waite
of Henley, Oxon b.1952
Adrian Pellew-Harvey 1967-94
Warren Pellew-Harvey b.1978
Alix b.1980
Jordan b.1982
Grace b.1983
Harriet b.1985
Clementine b.1988

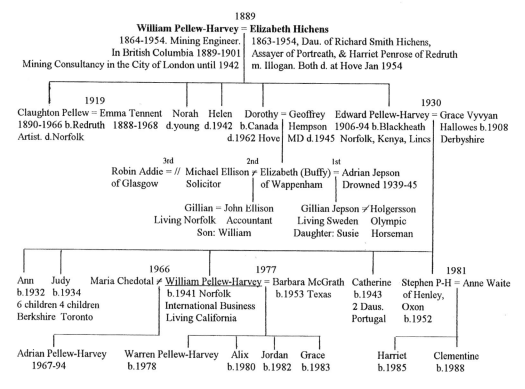

Descendants of William Pellew-Harvey & Elizabeth Hichens

Connects with the Harvey/Pellew chart on page 36

The departure of his family for Kenya in 1952 coincided with the start of the Mau Mau tribal insurrection in that country in which many native Kenyans and European settlers were to lose their lives. At the Prince of Wales School near Nairobi Bill found himself protected by barbed wire, sandbags and British troops in watch towers. Despite such restrictions life for a young boy in Kenya at that time was one of great freedom and Bill and the other sons of rural settlers were able to enjoy the excitements of that primitive, beautiful and sometimes savage land and its wildlife.

He was introduced to hunting by the Bowers, cousins of his mother, who leased a 50,000 acre ranch near Arusha in Tanganyika (Tanzania) at the foot of Mount Kilimanjaro. This is Africa's highest mountain (nearly 20,000 feet) which Bill and some school friends climbed in 1955. The ranch abounded in every type of big game and in those days there was hardly any poaching. "Trespassers were warned off and if they returned to poach were simply shot on sight" says Bill. Determined to become a "rancher" and settle permanently in Kenya, he left school at 15 and a year later in preparation for agricultural college was a student on an 8000 acre mixed arable and livestock farm in the high Kinankop. The owner was bedridden and, when the two farm managers left suddenly, Bill found himself managing the farm. He had to go about his business on horseback as he was too young to drive!

Fate intervened when he was offered the post of trainee at the head office of a French-owned ranching company at Ruiru. Bill had his father's charm and the general manager, Michel Huas who later became a director of the World Bank, took a liking to him and for two years saw to it that he learnt about accounting, company law and other skills needed in industrial management. So adept was the pupil that all thoughts of ranching evaporated and Bill's lifelong fascination with business began.

The dangers of hunting alone were demonstrated when Bill, aged 18, had to spend three months in hospital recovering from gunshot wounds. While camping near the Athi river 16 miles off the main Thika road he had been attacked by some roving Africans armed with pangas. They took his .22 rifle, shot him with it in the upper chest, stole his money and left him for dead. It was fortunate that despite heavy bleeding and a paralysed right arm he managed to drive in the dark to a house nearby.

In 1960 Bill's future in Kenya was finally determined by two events in the run up to independence at a time when the political climate was distinctly anti-European. One day as part of his duties he was patrolling a remote coffee plantation on the edge of a native reserve when he was confronted by a mob of angry and very menacing Wakamba tribesmen armed with spears and bows. He opened fire over their heads and, when this failed to stop them, shot into the ground in front of the ringleader. This dispersed the mob but Bill had later to appear before the magistrates for wounding the ringleader whose ear had been cut. He was acquitted, but within weeks was in trouble again when it was found that the girlfriend with whom he was living was a minor. The case was eventually dropped but it was clearly time to leave for Europe and a new career in business.

In London Bill joined one of its famous old trading houses, Henry W Peabody & Co, and for nearly four years travelled for them in Europe and the USA. Like the pied piper he built up such personal loyalty among his customers with his charm, energy and natural acumen that many of them followed him when he left Peabody to start his own first venture in the food industry. Based in Vancouver, his grandfather William's old stamping ground 70 years before, he purchased salmon all along the Pacific coast between Oregon and Alaska for sale in Europe. This soon became a seafood business with suppliers throughout the Far East, and Bill was able to invest in exotic automobiles, London night life and a wife, Maria Chedotal another Kenyan immigrant. She lived with this travelling dynamo for ten years and then left him with the parting words, "you are great fun to live with but a terrible husband!".

Bill Pellew-Harvey c. 1983

Meanwhile Bill's father on returning from Kenya had joined Pellew-Harvey & Co. It had grown into the largest independent frozen food distributor in UK when in 1974 Bill was forced to sell out to Christian Salvesen. Two years later by a stroke of fortune he bought forward Canada's export production of frozen potatoes and saw the market rise fourfold in three months. He used the handsome profits he made to enter a very different market. 'French fries' were replaced by security and defence equipment!

While these changes were in train Bill, who has a weakness for rash but romantic ventures, became involved in an unusual project in northern Thailand. This was a UN sponsored attempt to wean the poppy producers of the Golden Triangle off opium by helping them to grow other cash crops instead. Food processing plants had been established at Ching Mai, and Bill accompanied some of the UN teams on foot to help encourage the villagers in these remote lawless areas to cooperate with the scheme. They just proceeded to plant two crops instead of one, vegetables <u>and</u> opium! However it gave Bill the chance to visit one of the less accessible parts of the world and in the process do a bit of hunting for the pot.

In 1977 Bill married a new wife, a beautiful red-haired Texan, Barbara McGrath. She must be from strong frontier stock for Barbara in the first seven years of her married life gave birth to four children and set up five homes - in a London flat, a beautiful Maltese palazzo in the ancient city of Mdina, a flat in Rome, two conjoined apartments on the seafront at Monte Carlo and a large bungalow in a French village near Lake Geneva. The family now live in Mill Valley, California.

Meanwhile in Bill's new company, Bonaventure, the small team in London had been strengthened by the return from South Africa of his younger brother, Stephen. The company had had several lean years selling security equipment, night vision aids, pinhole cameras, bug detectors and the like, but in 1978 obtained a spectacularly large order for mine detectors from the oil-rich but trigger-happy dictatorship of Libya whose deserts are still littered with the debris of the campaigns of World War II. This change in fortunes was entirely due to Bill's opportunism, persistence and extraordinary patience and it led to further substantial contracts to supply other military materiel, civilian goods and services, and to the establishment of an office in Tripoli. Unfortunately Libya became a diminishing market as oil prices fell. They collapsed in 1984 and the Bonaventure operation there ceased and its London office closed.

Bill then began operating out of Geneva and with his Libyan experience it was not long before he was representing several European companies trying to sell defence equipment into Iran at the height of its long war against Iraq. He recalls that in Tehran his nights were spent either admiring anti-aircraft fire from the roof of his hotel or sheltering from the bombing in the basement of the Italian embassy. Neither physically nor politically was this a comfortable situation for one who had developed strong Arab ties after his six years in north Africa, and so by 1986 we find him taking root in Cairo, negotiating the supply of European armaments to the anti-Communist forces in Afghanistan. Two years later, after Western support had swung behind Iraq to prevent Iranian domination of the Gulf, he came full circle and was commuting to Baghdad!

His business in Iraq prospered even after the war ceased the following year. But it was a phoney peace which ended in August 1990 when Saddam Hussein invaded Kuwait. Fortunately Bill and his expatriate workers then happened to be out of Iraq except for one poor Frenchman whose release was negotiated some three weeks later. The embargo on sales to Iraq caused Bill to shut down in Geneva and lodge "massive claims" for compensation with the United Nations who imposed it. He tells me they have still to be met.

Ever the resilient trader, Bill with his wife Barbara then bought into an Italian mineral water plant called Solé - a rather less lethal commodity this time! They marketed it in the United States, where the family moved in 1993, and two years later successfully sold their holdings. Bill is now trading again, this time in central Asia opening yet another chapter in his business life. He is in a former region of the Soviet Union, the Kyrghyz Republic[9], where he says there are great opportunities.

---

[9] The Kyrghyz Republic (also known as Kyrghyzstan) is a mountainous state in the south of the old USSR and has a 500 mile border with Sinkiang, the western province of China.

BIBLIOGRAPHY

1. *The Story of Cornwall*, by S. Daniell, Tor Mark Press (1989)

2. *Enchanted Cornwall*, by Daphne du Maurier, Penguin Group (1989)

3. *A Retiring Fellow* by William Donaldson, BBC Radio 4 Broadcast (10 April 1996)

4. *The Story of Truro Cathedral*, by H. Miles Brown, Tor Mark Press (1991)

5. *Folklore & Legends of Cornwall*, by MA. Courtney, Cornwall Books (1989), Facsimile Edition of *Cornish Feasts & Folklore* (1890)

6. *The Cornish Mining Industry*, by JA. Buckley, Tor Mark Press (1995)

7. *A History of Copper Mining in Cornwall & Devon*, by DB. Barton (1961)

8. *Cornwall's Engine Houses*, by DB. Barton, Tor Mark Press (1994)

9. *Stannary Tales*, by Justin Brooke

10. *The History of Gwennap*, by CC. James

11. *The Mines of Cornwall - iv The Redruth Area*, by T. Spargo (1865)

12. *Last Stand against Home Counties Forces*, by Brian Jackman, Daily Telegraph (26 June 1997)

13. *California's Cornish Heritage*, CFHS Journal (June 1993)

14. *Heredity and Familial Disease*, Lecture by Dr. Ann Dally, Research Fellow of the Wellcome Institute (1993)

15. *Inherited Ability*, Lecture by Professor Joan Freeman, London University Institute of Education (1993)

16. *Facing the Sea*, by Nigel Tangye, William Kimber (1974)

17. *The Pellowes of Penryn*, by Dr. EF. Pellowe (1965)

18. *Edward Pellew, Viscount Exmouth, Admiral of the Red*, by C. Northcote Parkinson, Methuen (1934)

19. *The Life of Admiral Viscount Exmouth*, by Edward Osler, Smith Elder (1835)

20. *Royal Naval Biography 1823-24, Vol.1*, by J. Marshall

21. *Autobiography of James Silk Buckingham, Vol.1*, Longmans (1855)

BIBLIOGRAPHY (Continued)

22. O'Byrne's *Naval Biographical Dictionary*

23. Ralfe's *Naval Biography Vol.2* - Admiral Sir Israel Pellew

24. 'Obituary - Adm. Sir Israel Pellew', *Gentleman's Magazine ii 179* (1832)

25. *History of Shipwrecks, 2 s i*, by Cyrus Reddings (1835)

26. *Shipwrecks & Disasters at Sea Vol.3* - Explosion of the Frigate Amphion 1796

27. *The Story of Flushing*, by Ursula Redwood (1967)

28. *Trefusis Territory*, by Ursula Redwood (1987)

29. *The Sea Officer*, by Showell Styles, Faber & Faber (1961)

30. *The Visitation of England & Wales, Vol.21*, edited by FA. Crisp (1921)

31. *The Stock Exchange: Its History and Functions*, by EV. Morgan & WA. Thomas, London, 2nd Edn. (1969)

32. *Dictionary of British Surnames*, by P. Reaney, 2nd Edn. (1976)

33. *Collectanea Cornubiensia*, by GC Boase (1890)

34. *Bibliotheca Cornubiensus*, by Boase & Courtney

35. *Outline, An Autobiography & Other Writings* by Paul Nash, Faber & Faber (1949)

36. *Introduction to the Claughton Pellew Memorial Exhibition at Norwich* by John Nash (July 1967)

37. *Introduction to the 1990 Claughton Pellew Exhibition Catalogue* by Dr Andrew Causey, Hove Museum & Art Gallery (1990)

INDEX

INDEX

INDEX

INDEX

INDEX